A Call to Action

A Call to Action

Identification and Intervention for Twice and Thrice Exceptional Students

Blanche E. Sosland

ROWMAN & LITTLEFIELD

Lanham • Boulder • New York • London

Published by Rowman & Littlefield
An imprint of The Rowman & Littlefield Publishing Group, Inc.
4501 Forbes Boulevard, Suite 200, Lanham, Maryland 20706
www.rowman.com

86-90 Paul Street, London EC2A 4NE, United Kingdom

British Library Cataloguing in Publication Information Available

Library of Congress Cataloging-in-Publication Data

Names: Sosland, Blanche E. (Blanche Eisemann), 1936- author.
Title: A call to action : identification and intervention for twice and thrice exceptional students / Blanche E. Sosland.
Description: Lanham, Maryland : Rowman & Littlefield, 2022. | Includes bibliographical references and index. | Summary: "Educators, school administrators, counselors, and parents must have the necessary knowledge and understanding about twice exceptional students in order to be able to identify them and to provide meaningful academic and psycho-social interventions. A Call to Action provides tools to challenge these students' gifts and remediate their disabilities"—Provided by publisher.
Identifiers: LCCN 2021048590 (print) | LCCN 2021048591 (ebook) | ISBN 9781475864274 (cloth) | ISBN 9781475864281 (paperback) | ISBN 9781475864298 (epub)
Subjects: LCSH: Special education—Evaluation. | Exceptional children—Identification. | Children with disabilities—Education—Evaluation.
Classification: LCC LC3965 .S6414 2022 (print) | LCC LC3965 (ebook) | DDC 371.9—dc23/eng/20211109
LC record available at https://lccn.loc.gov/2021048590
LC ebook record available at https://lccn.loc.gov/2021048591

♾™ The paper used in this publication meets the minimum requirements of American National Standard for Information Sciences—Permanence of Paper for Printed Library Materials, ANSI/NISO Z39.48-1992.

Dr. Arthur Franklin Fost
November 3, 1936–August 17, 2021

*Beloved husband, father, grandfather, brother,
brother by marriage and uncle, physician*

Art volunteered globally delivering health care and teaching medicine in Ethiopia, Rwanda, Zaire, Tanzania, Israel, Guatemala, and El Salvador. Art cared for a large practice comprised of multiple generations of loyal patients.

The following story "says it all about Dr. Art."

When he and his wife, Ruth, went to get their COVID-19 vaccine a few months ago, a nurse administering shots a few booths away called out, "Dr. Fost! Dr. Fost! You probably don't remember me, but twenty years ago when I was a nursing student, and a patient of yours, I was crestfallen because I needed a series of allergy shots and couldn't afford them. When I told you this, without missing a beat you said, 'Oh, well today is your lucky day. We're having a special, free allergy shots for nursing students.'"

This story speaks about Dr. Art's quick wit and his joy in being a doctor and helping others in any way he could. It has been repeated in a thousand different ways of his fifty-five-year medical practice.

May his memory be for a blessing.

Contents

Foreword   ix

Preface   xi

Acknowledgments   xiii

1   Characteristics of Twice Exceptional Students   1

2   Identification of Twice Exceptional Students   13

3   Early Intervention   23

4   Informal Reading Inventory   33

5   Stopwatch Spelling   43

6   Twice Exceptional Students: Natural Aptitudes   53

7   Thrice Exceptional Students' Challenges   61

8   "Thou Shalt Not Bully"   71

9   Parent-Teacher Partnership   83

10   Creating a Path to Success for Twice Exceptional Students   93

Appendix A   103

Appendix B	107
References	109
Index	113
About the Author	119

Foreword

As a professor of family science and the parent of a twice exceptional child, this book resonates at both professional and personal levels. By sharing examples from years of work with educators, parents, and students, Blanche Sosland provides pathways to success for twice exceptional and thrice exceptional children and reassurance to families who are beginning that journey to know that success is in their reach.

This book reveals the roadblocks to remediation, the anxieties that children experience as a result, and then gives clear solutions that children need to build confidence, succeed academically, and achieve their life goals.

We need to join together as proud advocates and supporters of twice and thrice exceptional children in order to help build their capacity to feel successful. It is a call to action for all of us — students, parents, and professionals — to familiarize ourselves with these diagnostic and reading interventions that have demonstrated effective impact, but also to value different learning styles and support children's diverse needs in and out of the classroom.

Although twice and thrice exceptional children share many characteristics, they each have individual natural abilities, multiple intelligences, and learning challenges that will enable them to become successful students and adults.

— Elisabeth Maring,
Associate Clinical Professor,
University of Maryland School of Public Health

Preface

This urgent *Call to Action* is vital to assure that every student at grade level, exceptional, twice exceptional, thrice exceptional, and special needs can succeed academically and reflect on his/her school days with the wonderful recollections that Christina Sullivan has shared with us. There are roads to success for all students. We must help them travel those roads with confidence and show them how to succeed.

CHRISTINA'S WONDERFUL RECOLLECTIONS

"I had a great experience! I was in the Gifted/ Talented Program in KCMO from third to fifth grades. I have an older sister who would play school with me once she started school. So basically, I was learning what she could remember she learned each day. By the time I was in kindergarten, I was reading to the class upside down at story time and going to a first-grade class for my reading lesson.

"I don't remember taking any tests to determine anything. I think that my teachers just *observed* that I was getting bored and *worked quickly*. I usually finished class assignments and tests first and completed home-work before leaving class.

"Going to higher grades for instruction in certain subjects continued until third grade. I am not sure, but that may have been when they introduced the Gifted/Talented Program. I remember being taken out of class in the third grade to do some science experiments and other things. In fourth grade I was in a gifted/talented class. Then I was put in a combined fifth and sixth-grade gifted/talented class combined because there were not enough students in either grade to have separate classes.

"At that time, I also went down to the kindergarten to tutor students in reading and learning the alphabet. I think I only had one student I worked with. Then I went to the Kansas City Middle School of the Arts where we had wonderful teachers who taught us about learning styles and tried to meet the academic needs of each student.

"We also learned about how we needed so many hugs every day as a human to survive and grow. 'I am still friends with some of my high school teachers on Facebook today and I've been out of school for a while now'."

Christina highlighted what was the pathway to her academic success by having the needs of her exceptionality, gifted/talented met. The chapters that follow create a roadmap for parents, teachers, and students: exceptional, twice exceptional, thrice exceptional, special needs, and grade level as they embark on this journey of life-long learning.

Carl Sabatino, Publisher, and Chris Wiebe, Ed.D., Managing Editor of Variations2e, have given voice to scholars and educators who explore the intersections of race, culture, giftedness, and twice exceptionality. They have devoted the Summer 2021 edition of Variations2e to twice exceptionality and thrice exceptionalities. These voices must be heeded, understood, and responded to with appropriate action.

Some of the stories are heart-wrenching, others contain staggering statistics of inequities, all demand our attention and action. We must ask ourselves: how can we make a difference in our classrooms and in our homes? Each chapter is introduced with discussion points to involve readers, educators, and parents, to actively consider the answer to how we can make a difference.

This is our call to action!

Acknowledgments

To Tom Koerner of Rowman & Littlefield go my sincere and heartfelt thanks for always being there across these many miles, with the correct answer to all questions, large or small.

My sincere thanks to Kira Hall, assistant editor, Nivethitha Tamilselvan and Jade Bair for their ready answers to questions that arose during the writing process.

It is Josh Sosland's ability to find just the right word or phrase that has greatly enhanced the quality of this book. I am most appreciative of his professional guidance and encouragement.

David Sosland has been there night and day to help with the technology issues as they arose during the writing process of all four of my books. His knowledge, skill, and patience are so helpful and appreciated. Christina Sullivan's enormous talent as a graphic designer has added so much to the message of this book.

My appreciation to Dr. Don Breckon, Professor Elisabeth Maring, and Robbie Rothman Rice Bossart for reading parts of the manuscript and sharing their insights with me.

My gratitude goes to Tim Fitzgerald for answering my many questions concerning natural aptitudes.

My sincere appreciation to Jane Clementi for her very important edits.

Dr. Deborah Sosland-Edelman and Alan Edelman, Josh and Dr. Jane Mailman Sosland, Abby Sosland, J.D., and Mark Goodman, Dr. Jeffrey

Karl Sosland and Mindy Sosland, David and Dr. Rachel Sosland, so grateful for your tremendous support and inspiration you provide.

And to the next generations, Alex, Katja, Ari, Jonathan, Sam, Max, Leah, Sophie, Lily, Zachary, Kate, Henry, Ethan, Gabrielle, Jake, and Juliet, congratulations on your many accomplishments so early in your lives. And to Noa, Kobi, and Rahm, you are pure joy.

To my quintessential husband thanks for love,
friendship, and sharing "the best is yet to come."

Chapter 1

Characteristics of Twice Exceptional Students

INTRODUCTION

EDUCATORS

1. Which of these characteristics do you find most often among your twice exceptional students?

2. Discuss how you address these characteristics.

PARENTS

1. Which of these characteristics describe your child?

2. How do you address those characteristics?

As Thad's mother was walking to the pond to feed the ducks, she overheard him discussing Moby Dick with Evan. The two boys were sitting on the side of the swimming pool on a hot summer day. The family lived in an updated French provincial farmhouse on several acres in North Jersey.

She was somewhat surprised that her five-year-old son knew about Moby Dick and that he was able to discuss it with eighteen-year-old Evan, his cousin who was visiting for a week. She didn't give it too much thought at the time, but it became an important recollection when Thad was still having difficulty learning to read at age seven in second grade. It assured her that he was not developmentally delayed.

She asked him how he knew about Moby Dick, and he told her that he had watched the movie on television. The fact that he was interested in that movie at that young age and understood enough to be able to discuss it with an eighteen-year-old was a strong indication that he might be twice exceptional.

His school recommended that he undergo an Educational Evaluation that in turn documented the fact that he was twice exceptional. He scored in the Superior range in intelligence, three years above his age in oral language while disabled by dyslexia. Working through his strengths and challenging his intellect he also continued his remedial reading program. Listening to audiobooks three years beyond his grade level was very important to keep him intellectually challenged.

One of the greatest challenges faced by classroom teachers is *the identification of learners with diverse needs*, and one of the greatest sources of professional satisfaction is the ability to meet these diverse needs successfully. Learners with diverse needs include students who are reading below grade level and yet not far enough below to qualify for remedial reading instruction, students who are functioning above grade level and yet do not meet the guidelines for a gifted/talented program, and those students who are twice exceptional (2e) both learning disabled and gifted/talented.

Although twice exceptional students exhibit many characteristics of both gifted and learning-disabled students, they are often the most difficult to identify because the disability may mask the giftedness and the giftedness may mask the disability. Thus, neither exceptionality is addressed, leading to frustration on the part of the student, the parents, and the teacher. This often manifests itself through behavior problems in the classroom and/or at home.

An estimated 6 percent of the students in special educations have been identified as twice exceptional. An estimated 300,000–360,000 of all students have been identified to be twice exceptional. Because of the difficulty identifying these students, this estimate is probably low. With the growing recognition of the special needs of 2e students, advocacy groups are organizing to support teacher training programs to assure all faculty members meet the needs of these students.

In order for classroom teachers to be able to meet the individual needs of each of these students, they must understand that they can, in fact, screen for certain reading difficulties experienced by students who would otherwise "fall through the cracks." One of the most valuable diagnostic tools available to classroom teachers is the Informal Reading Inventory. Therefore, a chapter in this book is devoted to preparing all preservice teachers to enter the classroom equipped to use this diagnostic instrument effectively.

Zack, a twice exceptional student, was in the second grade. His reading at the Instructional Level was established at the first-grade level, thus a full level below grade level, and his Listening Capacity Level was at the sixth-grade level. Zack's reading difficulty masked his giftedness, that is, his ability to comprehend reading material four grade levels beyond his grade level when that material was read to him. This led to enormous frustration and Zack became a behavior problem. Zack required remedial reading instruction to bring him up to his intellectual capacity and he needed enrichment to challenge his intellectual strength. Zack is the classic example of a twice exceptional student and how he/she can be identified.

Zack's teacher provided audiobooks at the sixth-grade level in the Classroom Listening Center, keeping Zack intellectually challenged. The Informal Reading Inventory identified the areas of reading instruction in which Zack required tutoring to be brought up to his intellectual level. A volunteer tutor gave him that instruction.

A few examples of famous people who were twice exceptional and able to achieve enormous success because of their ability to compensate for their learning disabilities include Presidents George Washington and Woodrow Wilson, Tom Cruise, an actor, Patricia Polacco, author and artist, and Vice-President Nelson Rockefeller. These individuals were all dyslexic. Nelson Rockefeller who was also governor of New York is said to have memorized every speech because of concern about his inability to read the words. Individuals in every field of endeavor include Winston Churchill, world leader; Walt Disney, artist, a pioneer in Hollywood films and television as well as a folk hero of the twentieth century who represented imagination, optimism, and self-made success in the American tradition; Alexander Graham Bell, inventor; and Thomas Edison, one of the world's most prolific inventors holding over one thousand United States patents, all had specific learning disabilities. Edison was also dyslexic and didn't learn to read until he was twelve years old.

In school, the young Edison's mind often wandered, and his teacher, the Reverend Engle, was overheard calling him "addled." This ended Edison's three months of official schooling. Edison recalled later, "My mother was the making of me. She was so true, so sure of me, and I felt I had something to live for, someone I must not disappoint." His mother home-schooled him.

Patricia Polacco, who didn't learn to read until she was fourteen and didn't write the first of her almost fifty books until the age of forty-one, truly helps us understand the struggles and pain of the twice exceptional child. Her autobiographical "Thank You Mr. Falker" is dedicated to George Falker, the real Mr. Falker, "a teacher who unlocked the door and pulled (her) into the light."

Once she learned to read, all Polacco wanted was to be in a class of "regular" students. She was devastated when she discovered that she had been assigned to the class known in her new school as "the junkyard." Mrs. Peterson is the teacher of this class of twice exceptional students and the heroine of "The Junkyard Wonders." In the epilogue, we read the success stories of the "junkyard" students including the artistic director of the American Ballet Theater Company in New York, a textile designer in Paris, and an aeronautical engineer for NASA who helped design the lunar modules for the Apollo missions.

Although both books are written for children of all ages, adults, including parents and educators, enjoy and appreciate them as well. Patricia Polacco devotes much of her time speaking to school audiences to convey her admiration and appreciation for what teachers accomplish.

The US Department of Education, Office of Civil Rights, began to collect data about ten years ago on the number of K-12 students identified as gifted/talented and receiving services for a learning disability. In the Individuals with Learning Disabilities Educational Act (IDEA) these students are identified as having "A disorder in one or more of the basic psychological processes involved in understanding or in using language spoken or written, which may manifest itself in an imperfect ability to listen, speak, read, write, spell or do mathematical calculations."

In spite of the fact that this group of children is so diverse, they share many characteristics that should help parents and teachers identify them and provide the interventions to enable them to achieve academic success. In addition, it is important for pediatricians and other health care providers to be able to identify these twice exceptional children as well. Physicians often make significant recommendations to parents that enable their children to achieve success in school.

CHARACTERISTICS OF TWICE EXCEPTIONAL STUDENTS

- They perform well in some classes and poorly in others. They perform well in the area of their giftedness but do poorly in the area affected by their learning disability.
- Many twice exceptional students do poorly at rote memorization.
- They have difficulty completing easy assignments but do well with more difficult concepts.
- These students have periods of "spaciness" or "glazed look" during which time they are in deep thought.
- One of the most perplexing characteristics is that they can be hyperactive at times but also have periods of deep concentration to the point that they shut out the rest of the world.
- Many of these students do not perform well on timed tests because they analyze the questions to a much greater depth than the average student.
- Problems with eye-hand coordination or fine motor skills make it difficult for some 2e students to take notes in class.

STRENGTHS AND WEAKNESSES OF TWICE EXCEPTIONAL STUDENTS

- Twice exceptional children often have much stronger oral language in contrast to their written language. They think in higher level concepts and as mentioned above they do not do well with rote memorization. This contrast between oral and written language is a strong indicator of 2e and is readily observable.

- Their long-term memory is much stronger than their short-term memory. These contrasts are also readily observable by both parents and teachers.
- Twice exceptional students have difficulty learning basic skills in contrast to higher level creative tasks because of cognitive processing difficulties.
- Some 2e students are leaders, others are socially awkward and isolated.

It is really important to focus on the twice exceptional child's strengths. There is significant research that supports the importance of developing children's interests, challenging their intellect, and encouraging abstract thinking and creativity. In contrast, research reports that focus on weakness and learning disability can result in poor self-esteem, lack of motivation, stress, anxiety, and depression.

Educators have long understood that children learn in different ways using different modalities. Therefore, many have embraced Howard Gardner's Multiple Intelligences. Gardner questioned why so many individuals were just average students throughout the school and yet became enormously successful in adult life. He concluded that success in school was measured primarily by strength in linguistic and logical-mathematical intelligence while success in adult life includes spatial, bodily-kinesthetic, musical, interpersonal, intrapersonal, and naturalistic intelligences (see table 1.1).

Linguistic Intelligence is the ability to use words effectively — the written word as well as oral language. Much of the school curriculum is devoted to the development of this intelligence. It is the intelligence used by the author, public speaker, and, in everyday life, the ability to read traffic signs and recipes.

Logical-mathematical Intelligence is the capacity to work well with numbers and/or to have talent using logic or reasoning. This is the intelligence of scientists, accountants, computer programmers and also a major factor in school success.

Spatial Intelligence involves the ability to visualize pictures in one's head or to create them. Artists, sculptors, and inventors make strong use of this intelligence. Einstein said that he used this intelligence to come up with his theories of relativity.

Bodily-kinesthetic Intelligence is the intelligence of the whole body including the hands. Einstein wrote that in addition to visual and spatial capacities, he also used "muscular" processes in working out some of his top physics problems. It covers a broad range of professions from athlete and actor to machinist and surgeon. In everyday life, it includes actions from using a can opener to playing a strong game of tennis.

Musical Intelligence includes the ability to carry a tune, remember melodies, a sense of rhythm, talent to compose music, or to just enjoy listening to music. Students who are strong in Musical Intelligence often are unaware that they tap their feet while doing their classwork. Musical Intelligence is also used in a wide variety of careers ranging from the performing arts to piano tuners to music therapists.

Interpersonal Intelligence is a talent for working well with people. As students, they often are not too successful academically because they are too busy socializing but become enormously successful in the business world.

Thomas Armstrong, himself twice exceptional, suggests that strong *Intrapersonal Intelligence* "may be the hardest to fully understand but it also could very well be the most important . . . It is essentially the intelligence of self-understanding, of knowing who you are." This is an

Table 1.1   Howard Gardner's Multiple Intelligences

1. **LINGUISTIC INTELLIGENCE** The ability to use words effectively, the written word as well as oral language.
2. **LOGICAL-MATHEMATICAL INTELLIGENCE** The capacity to work well with numbers and/or to have talent using logic or reasoning.
3. **SPATIAL INTELLIGENCE** The ability to visualize pictures in one's head or to create them.
4. **BODILY-KINESTHETIC INTELLIGENCE** The intelligence of the whole body including the hands.
5. **MUSICAL INTELLIGENCE** The ability to carry a tune, remember melodies, have a sense of rhythm, talent to compose music, or to just enjoy listening to music.
6. **INTERPERSONAL INTELLIGENCE** A talent for working well with people.
7. **INTRAPERSONAL INTELLIGENCE** The intelligence of self-understanding.
8. **NATURALISTIC INTELLIGENCE** The ability to identify natural forms around us.

important intelligence for counselors and therapists to help others get a better understanding of themselves.

Naturalist Intelligence involves the ability to identify natural forms around us such as flora and fauna, geological formations, and cloud formations. It is the intelligences of the biologist, forest ranger, and veterinarian.

Gardner stresses that everyone possesses all eight intelligences in varying degrees. There are many instruments readily available on the internet for parents and educators to assess each child's level of intelligence among the eight and then to focus on the strongest intelligences to work through strength. For example, children who are gifted in Musical Intelligence are often also very strong in Logical-mathematical Intelligence but may have a learning disability in the area of Linguistic Intelligence. They should be taught through their strong intelligences and to compensate in their weaker area. Thus, opportunities to have music lessons, participate in musical groups such as bands and/or orchestras, science fairs will allow these 2e children to experience success and build self-esteem.

As discussed earlier, teaching to the strengths is the most effective way to help students compensate for their learning deficit. Identifying each child's interests is another key factor to enable the child to compensate. Establishing whether the child learns best using auditory, visual, or kinesthetic approach is also very important.

For many twice exceptional children getting their thoughts from their head to the paper is a major stumbling block. Having them practice developing their handwriting skills should be done in no more than fifteen-minute increments whether at school or at home. Permission to use computers for writing tasks has been a very effective means for 2e students to compensate.

For some twice exceptional students it is helpful to learn the use of mnemonics and/or visualization. Knowing that 2e students do well learning complex abstract concepts they should be given the opportunity to do so.

The first step, and often the most challenging, to help twice exceptional students succeed in school commensurate with their abilities to identify them. Once this is done their giftedness can be addressed as well as intervention for their learning disabilities can proceed. From there, not only can they be successful, but they can also go to the moon. Patricia Polacco's "junkyard wonders" did just that and we can be certain we got to Mars with the genius of a number of twice exceptional students.

Another of the major stumbling blocks in the identification process is the fact that in many school districts students who test at grade level on standardized tests will not qualify for special services. Thus, when the learning disability brings the gifted/talented score down to grade level, these students receive neither special services nor individualized attention in the classroom. That is the reason all classroom teachers must use the various instruments discussed in this book to provide the proper instruction for their 2e students.

The top ten private schools in the United States designed for twice exceptional students are described online. For example, they have one classroom with bare white walls to accommodate the students who are easily distracted and a different classroom with brightly colored pictures and decor for students who need stimulation. Each student's curriculum is individualized, and they are taught in small groups with no class larger than ten.

Not too many families can afford the cost of 2e private education which at the time of this writing was $79,250.00. Many of the families are suing the Department of Education for not meeting the educational needs of their children. This is also costly and the money the government spends to pay these lawsuits, 2e advocates point out would be much better spent on training teachers and for the development of public-school teachers.

Many teachers design their classrooms with a "space" where students can go for quiet time if they feel they need it. The "space" might be painted a different color from the rest of the classroom, to make it special, and might be called "Cozy Corner" or "The Office" or "Mars" or anything the class decides on. This author actually saw one classroom where the teacher and her students built a treehouse in the classroom for students to take turns on as a special reward during free reading time.

A Listening Center could accommodate the Musical Intelligence of students who have that intellectual strength. There should be a center to fulfill the needs of students who excel in each of Howard Gardner's Multiple Intelligences.

This chapter was designed to establish the foundation for every classroom teacher to meet the challenge of identifying and educating the diverse intellectual backgrounds of his/her students. Given the challenge of identifying twice exceptional students, it is important for teachers to have the classroom instruments to enable them to do so, as well as knowledge of the characteristics of these very special students.

The following chapters will enable classroom teachers to *show* their students that in fact they *can* learn in spite of their disability and that they can soar because of their gift/talent. As teachers, we learn much from our students.

There was an important lesson the author learned from an eighth-grade student she tutored as part of a special University remedial reading program. The student had gained five reading grade levels in sixteen weeks. When asked how she was able to do that she replied, "You *showed* me I could read. Everyone else had given up on me." *We cannot and must not give up on any student!* Identification and early intervention enable us to help our students succeed.

CHAPTER 1. CHARACTERISTICS OF TWICE EXCEPTIONAL STUDENTS

Post

EDUCATORS: FOR CLASS DISCUSSION

1. Which of these characteristics do you find most often among your twice exceptional students?

2. Compare and contrast the characteristics you find most often with those found by your classmates/colleagues.

3. Discuss how you address these characteristics.

PARENTS

1. Which of these characteristics describe your child?

2. Are there any additional characteristics based on your reading of the chapter?

3. Will you make any changes as to how you address those characteristics?

Chapter 2

Identification of Twice Exceptional Students

INTRODUCTION

EDUCATORS

1. Describe how you will identify the twice exceptional students in your classroom.

2. Discuss the importance of the identification of twice and thrice exceptional students.

PARENTS

1. Discuss how you will advocate for the identification of your child's twice exceptionality.

2. How did you identify your child's twice exceptionality?

Annie was a fourth-grade student who should have been in the fifth grade. She was retained in the first grade. Annie was being instructed at the second-grade reading level based on her scores on a standardized test.

Annie's teacher called the Education Department at Park University to inquire about the availability of a student to tutor Annie. Her teacher explained that Annie was not making any progress and she thought working one-on-one with an education major might be effective.

Annie was matched with a Park University senior during her practicum because Annie's outstanding teacher sensed and observed that there was something wrong with the interpretation of the results of the battery of tests that Annie had taken at the beginning of the school year.

Annie had been referred for testing and evaluation because a learning disability was suspected but not confirmed. Instead, the results indicated that Annie was a slow learner according to the scores on the standardized Wechsler IQ test.

The Park University tutor gave Annie an Informal Reading Inventory (IRI) and established that Annie scored as instructional at the pre-primer level. She had been instructed for five years at her Frustration Level. The end result was that her IQ had dropped fourteen points from the normal range she had scored in first grade to the slow range. The evaluation also indicated that anxiety was interfering with Annie's learning.

Annie had been diagnosed with a learning disability in first grade. That was the reason given for holding her back a year. She is a prime example of why students should not be instructed at their Frustration Level.

Annie's score on the Listening Capacity portion of the IRI was at the fifth-grade level. This score is established after the student reaches his/ her Frustration Level and the teacher/tutor reads to the student and the student answers questions with 60 percent to 75 percent accuracy. Thus, it is clear that Annie is *capable* of doing grade-level work.

All this information was collected in approximately fifteen minutes by a preservice college senior. Given this information, Annie was instructed one-on-one by her tutor at her instructional level, pre-primer. Her tutor was able to demonstrate to Annie that she could teach Annie how to read and that Annie could really learn to read, a fact that Annie had learned to doubt for many years.

Within a matter of weeks, Annie had moved up a whole grade level in reading and when post-tested at the end of the eight-week practicum,

Annie had advanced three grade levels. After all these years, Annie was finally being retaught all the reading skills that she had missed because of learning disability. Although Annie is not a twice exceptional student, she is a special needs student and her story represents all special needs students, including 2e.

There are a number of points in Annie's story that illustrate the importance of identification for intervention. First, it was the ability of Annie's teacher to observe and identify a serious problem.

She knew that Annie was not a slow learner.

When asked how she knew Annie was not a slow learner even though standardized testing had identified her as such, Annie's teacher replied,

> I have been teaching for 15 years and I could tell by Annie's eyes that she is not a slow learner. Over the years I have seen the dull look in the eyes of my slow learners to be able to tell the difference. You don't have to be teaching 15 years to be able to tell the difference.

The second point is that there are many children in our classrooms who are experiencing delays in reading acquisition because of instruction that may have been inappropriate for them.

At the University of Missouri-Kansas City Reading Clinic, 80 percent to 85 percent of the students enrolled are taught to read by simply identifying their deficits and reteaching them the necessary skills.

That would seem to indicate that the original instruction was not appropriate for them when it was introduced or that they were not ready for the instruction. In Annie's case, she was being instructed at the second-grade level based on a standardized reading test that had a baseline at the second-grade and did not identify many earlier skills that were missing. Once these skills were identified and by reteaching them, Annie could make tremendous progress.

Most important of all Annie was shown that she, in fact, could learn to read. After all those years of failure and frustration, it is not surprising that she had given up. Her learning disability had been identified in first grade. Why she didn't receive the appropriate intervention is puzzling, but it is hoped that the lessons from her story will save other students from "falling through the cracks" as she did.

In order to meet the academic needs of twice exceptional children, it is necessary to identify their twice exceptionality. This can often be challenging because the giftedness might mask the learning disability and the learning disability might mask the giftedness. Then neither is addressed leading to frustration on the part of the child, the parents, and the teachers.

Twice exceptional children can fall into one of three categories:
1. The *unidentified* who was just described with one exceptionality masking the other.
2. *Identified gifted* child who has subtle learning disabilities. This is a very bright child, yet his/her achievement is not commensurate with his/her potential. This child's learning disability is so subtle that it goes unidentified, and parents and teachers are puzzled by the fact that the child is not achieving commensurate with his/her intellectual capacity.
3. *Identified learning-disabled* child who is also gifted. This child is identified because of his/her learning disability and the child's giftedness/talent is overlooked because of the learning disability.

There are numerous ways these 2e children can be identified as are other children with special needs. That is why Annie's story is so important. Her teacher's observation was key to finally establish Annie's intervention. Thus, we will start with teacher's observation.

An excellent paper on teacher's observation was published online a number of years ago and is still highly regarded in its field. "Teacher Observation in Student Assessment" was prepared for the Queensland School Curriculum by Graham S. Maxwell of the School of Education, the University of Queensland. Dr. Maxwell maintains that "A strong justification for using observation in assessment is its capacity to enhance assessment validity." By extending the range of possible assessments, teacher's observations allow assessments to be more:

- *Comprehensive* — ensuring recognition of all desired learning outcomes, especially those not otherwise assessable than in classroom contexts
- *Connected* — situated within familiar learning contexts and closely related to curriculum frameworks, learning experienced, and pedagogical planning
- *Contextualized* — sensitive to the effects of context on performance and deriving assessment evidence from a variety of situations and contexts

- *Authentic* — interesting, challenging, worthwhile, and meaningful to the students
- *Holistic* — emphasizing relatedness and connections in learning and involving performance on complex wholes rather than separate components

Dr. Maxwell and others in the field characterize teacher's observation as either incidental or planned. Incidental observation occurs when an unplanned opportunity arises during the course of regular daily instruction. Some question whether incidental observation can be used for formal assessment. Annie's teacher's observation might be considered incidental and yet was very powerful.

Planned observation, as the name indicates, is designed for the teacher to observe specific learning outcomes. It can take place in the regular classroom or in a different setting.

The IRI is a very important tool for the identification of twice exceptional students as well as all special needs students. For that reason, a whole chapter has been devoted to one specific IRI — the Classroom Reading Inventory that has one part to establish the Listening Capacity. The information is vital, the key to the identification of 2e and special needs students.

The concept of the IRI goes back a century to the 1920s. Professor Thorndike, Columbia University, is credited with the original concept, but it was not until the 1940s that Professor Emmett Betts of Temple University and Professor Nicholas Silvaroli actually published the first IRIs.

Since then, literally thousands of teachers, reading specialists, reading coaches, professionals in higher education, and those charged with the professional development of preservice and in-service teachers have created IRIs to meet their specific instructional assessment needs. Some Reading Education Majors are even encouraged to create their own IRI to get a better understanding of the reading process.

Not all twice exceptional share the same characteristics and behaviors. But research has shown that there are quite a few that parents and teachers report they observe in their 2e children and students. Sensitivity to these characteristics and behaviors is important to meeting their 2e needs (see table 2.1).

Table 2.1   Twice Exceptional Characteristics and Behaviors

CHARACTERISTICS AND BEHAVIORS	*IDEAS FOR SUCCESS*
Perform well in some classes and poorly in others	Parents and classroom teachers should be sure that these children are taught to use their strengths, interests, and learning styles. Visual, auditory, and kinesthetic approaches should be used. Computer-assisted instruction can be a very valuable tool for these children.
Does poorly at rote memorization and drill	These children should do these types of learning tasks in small increments. They should be taught to use mnemonics and visualization. Material should be presented in more complex, abstract concepts whenever possible.
Tripped up by easy assignments, does well with more difficult concepts	It is important that easy, sequential materials are eliminated and that these children are taught advanced material holistically.
Is easily distracted	Homework should be done in a quiet work area with no distractions. Classroom should also have a quiet work area. Earphones work well for some children.
Has difficulty with phonics	They should be taught through a whole word approach using sight words to learn to read. The *Language Experience Approach* can also be very effective.
Challenged by spelling lessons	They should then be taught to visualize their spelling words. Have them pretend that their brain is a camera. Close their eyes until they can see the spelling word. Have them write the word in the air and on paper and/or sand until each word is mastered.
Difficulty with math facts	They should be taught to make math charts and look for patterns.
Hyperactive or extended periods of deep concentration	It is very important for parents and teachers to be sensitive and responsive to these behaviors. In the classroom, the child should be allowed to move around quietly in the back of the room without disturbing his/her classmates. In such episodes it usually doesn't take long for the child to settle down and resume work. These children should be allowed to pursue their "passions" both at home and at school.
Periods of "spaciness" or a "glazed look"	Most classroom teachers find that by gently touching the child's shoulder they are able to get his/her attention back to the task at hand.
Difficulty following directions	Parents and teachers should be certain that they establish eye contact with their child/student before they give a direction. Teachers should also write the directions on paper and/or on the board. *(Continued)*

Table 2.1   Twice Exceptional Characteristics and Behaviors (*Continued*)

CHARACTERISTICS AND BEHAVIORS	IDEAS FOR SUCCESS
Illegible handwriting	Allowing these children to use a computer can be very helpful to compensate for this.
Does not do well on times tests	Schools should have a policy to allow these children to take tests untimed.
Note taking is a problem	Parents and teachers should be aware of the fact that note taking may be a problem for 2e children. They should be encouraged to use a computer or tablet. A "study buddy" system of sharing notes has proved to be helpful as well.

CHARACTERISTICS AND BEHAVIORS OF 2E

- *Twice exceptional students characteristically perform well in some classes and poorly in others.*

Parents and classroom teachers should be sure that these children are taught to their strengths, interests, and learning styles. Visual, auditory, and kinesthetic approaches should be used. Computer-assisted instruction can be a very valuable tool for these children.

- *2e children often do poorly at rote memorization and drill.*

These children should do these types of learning tasks in small increments. They should be taught to use mnemonics and visualization. The material should be presented in more complex, abstract concepts whenever possible.

- *Many 2e children have difficulty completing easy assignments but do well with more difficult concepts.*

It is important that easy, sequential materials are eliminated and that these children are taught advanced material holistically.

• *Some twice exceptional children are easily distracted.*

Homework should be done in a quiet work area with no distractions. Classroom should also have a quiet work area. Earphones work well for some children.

• *2e children may experience difficulty with phonics.*

They should then be taught through a whole word approach using sight words to learn to read. The Language Experience Approach can also be very effective.

• *Many 2e children experience difficulty with spelling.*

These children should be taught to visualize their spelling words. Have them pretend that their brain is a camera, close their eyes until they can see the spelling word, have them write the word in the air and on paper and/or sand until each word is mastered.

• *2e children experience difficulty with math facts.*

They should be taught to make math charts and look for patterns.

• *Twice exceptional children can be hyperactive at times and at other times can have periods of deep concentration.*

It is very important for parents and teachers to be sensitive and responsive to these behaviors. In the classroom, the child should be allowed to move around quietly in the back of the room without disturbing his/her classmates. Usually doesn't take long for the child to settle down and resume work. These children should be allowed to pursue their "passions" both at home and at school.

• *Periods of "spaciness" or that "glazed look" should be noted and addressed.*

Most classroom teachers find that by gently touching the child's shoulder, they are able to get his/her attention back to the task at hand.

- *Following directions can be difficult for some 2e children.*

Parents and teachers should be certain that they have eye contact with their child/student before they give a direction. It is very important that teachers should make eye contact with their 2e students before they begin to give directions. Teachers should also write the directions on paper and/or on the board.

- *Illegible handwriting is another characteristic shared by many 2e children.* Allowing these children to use a computer can be very helpful to compensate for this.
- *Many 2e children do not do well on timed tests.* Schools should have a policy to allow these children to take tests untimed.
- *Parents and teachers should be aware of the fact that note taking can be a problem for 2e children.* They should be encouraged to use a computer or tablet. A "study buddy" system of sharing notes has proved to be helpful as well.

It is so important for parents and teachers to work together to assure the academic success of their 2e children and students. Not every 2e child will experience all the challenges discussed above but identifying those that are relevant will help your child/student achieve academic success.

Identification of the relevant challenges for each child/student will enable you to create a nurturing learning environment at home and at school. Individual differences should be valued as a positive attribute and conveyed as such. The mutual support of home and school is very important to assure academic success for twice exceptional children as well as for all special needs children.

Again, it is really important to focus on every child's/student's strengths. Howard Gardner's "multiple intelligences" enables us to look for the genius in every child and to focus on every child's strength. In contrast, research has shown that a focus on weaknesses, learning disability can lead to behavior problems, poor self-esteem, a lack of motivation, stress, and depression.

CHAPTER 2. IDENTIFICATION OF
TWICE EXCEPTIONAL STUDENTS

Post

EDUCATORS

1. Discuss how you will identify the twice exceptional students in your classroom based on your reading of this chapter.

2. Discuss any new insights you might have on the importance of the identification of twice and thrice exceptional students.

PARENTS

1. Discuss how you will advocate for the identification of your child's twice exceptionality.

2. Do you have any additional ideas as how to advocate for the identification of your child's twice exceptionality based on this chapter?

3. How did you identify your child's twice exceptionality?

Chapter 3

Early Intervention

INTRODUCTION

EDUCATORS

1. Discuss how you plan to intervene on behalf of the twice exceptional children in your classroom.

2. Describe the learning environment you plan to create in your classroom.

3. Outline the type of interventions you plan to use for your gifted/talented students.

4. Outline the type of interventions you plan to accommodate the needs of your students who have learning disabilities.

PARENTS

1. How do you plan to advocate for your child's interventions?

2. How do you plan to support the interventions your child is receiving?

Going anywhere with dad was a special treat. With a family of six children ranging in age from fourteen to two, both parents tried to carve out one-on-one time with each child whenever possible. Dad needed a new pair of running shoes and decided to take two-year-old Jason with him. He walked to the mirror to check out the shoes, turned around and Jason was gone. Frantic, he ran around the store asking if anyone had seen a four-year-old.

At age two, Jason was so big that he looked like a four-year-old and sure enough a sales lady said she thought she saw him get into the elevator! Now the question was on which floor did he get off? An all-store alert located him on the fourth floor, having the best time exploring, totally unaware of all the panic he had caused!

Several years later his physical and mental maturity came into play once again. His mother shared the end-of-the-year letter she and her husband received from Jason's preschool teacher. She said she had received many nice end-of-the-year letters from preschool teachers for the older children, but this letter topped them all.

Montessori Preschool

Dear Mr. and Mrs. Star:

It was a pleasure and privilege to have Jason in my class this year. He is such a happy youngster and so well-liked by his classmates. Whenever we play a game where a child chooses another child to go next Jason is chosen the most often. At one point he said, "I think I have had enough turns and you should choose someone else." I have never had a five-year-old do that before.

Wishing Jason every success in kindergarten and beyond,
Warm Regards,
Betsy E. Peal

Within a few days of the beginning of kindergarten, Jason's mom started to receive phone calls about Jason's disruptive behavior in class. After the third or fourth call, she decided to call Jason's preschool teacher and said, "You sent us the most glowing end-of-the-year letter about Jason. All I am getting now is complaints about his behavior from his teacher. Can a child change that much over the summer?"

Mrs. Peal said she would visit Jason's class to observe him in that setting. She quickly realized why Jason was being disruptive. She and Jason had had an agreement. Whenever Jason needed to move around, he could go to the back of the room without disrupting the class and quietly move around until he was ready to settle down. She suggested that his kindergarten teacher make the same pact with him. She did and that ended the problem.

By second grade when he was still experiencing difficulty learning to read, his teacher recommended that Jason see a psychologist for an Educational Evaluation. The results of the evaluation were that Jason was twice exceptional. Once he received that diagnosis the appropriate interventions were applied.

The characteristics of twice exceptional students were discussed in chapter 1. The interventions for these characteristics will be discussed in this chapter. It is imperative for parents to advocate for their 2e children. Hopefully their classroom teachers will be using these interventions, but it cannot be stressed enough to note how important it is for parents and teachers to work together to assure the success of these children/students.

A meeting between parents and teachers at the beginning of the academic year should be scheduled to discuss the specific interventions for each child. Parents should come to the meeting prepared to learn how their child's teacher plans to address the specific needs of their child. Hopefully they will be applying the appropriate interventions from among the following discussion or one from their own repertoire of teaching strategies.

Parents should come to the meeting prepared to request specific interventions when necessary. If for some reason the teacher is not willing to incorporate these interventions parents must talk to the school administration to assure that their child's academic needs are met in the classroom, even if it is necessary to move your child to a classroom where the teacher will accommodate your child's academic needs.

These children are major contributors to our society as adults and should receive all the support they need in the classroom. After all, they have taken us to the Moon and Mars!

For the students who do well in some classrooms and poorly in others teaching should be directed at their strengths. Taken into consideration should be their natural aptitudes, multiple intelligences, and learning styles. There are ample assessment tools to determine these basic strengths and will be discussed in later chapters.

Visual, auditory, and kinesthetic approaches should be used so that all the modalities are incorporated in the learning process. Computer-assisted instruction can be a very valuable tool for these students.

Appropriate remediation should take place in the classes where these students perform poorly. Many twice exceptional children do poorly in reading and spelling; therefore, a whole chapter has been devoted to each topic in order for appropriate intervention to take place.

A high percentage of twice exceptional students experience difficulty with rote memorization and drill. They should be taught mnemonics and visualization. Visualization is taught very early when spelling is introduced. Somehow, many twice exceptional students don't grasp this instruction at that time and have to be retaught how to visualize when that gap is identified.

One technique is to have the students pretend that their brains are cameras and to take pictures of the spelling words. This will be discussed in more detail in chapter 5 and has been a very effective intervention.

Twice exceptional students also find it helpful to have information presented in more complex and abstract concepts and this is another way to work through their identified strengths. By the same token, they have difficulty completing assignments that are considered easy and do well with more challenging concepts.

Thus, it is important for parents as advocates for their twice exceptional children to be sure that the classroom teacher individualizes work enough so that easy, sequential material is eliminated from 2e instruction. It is important to challenge the gifted/talented exceptionality by instructing them with advanced material holistically.

Some twice exceptional children are easily distracted. They should be seated in the classroom where there will be the least distractions. In many cases, that is in the front row next to the teacher's desk. Homework should be done in a quiet area with no distractions. Earphones and pods work well for some of these children.

Another area that quite a few 2e students find challenging is phonics. They should be taught to read using a whole word approach. There are many published reading programs that use the whole word approach using sight words. The Language Experience Approach, using the student's own language, is also a very effective method to teach 2e students how to read.

Spelling is a problem for many twice exceptional children. So much so, a whole chapter has been devoted to it. Briefly, in many cases it is necessary to reteach students how to visualize their spelling words. Have them close their eyes until they can see the spelling word. Then they write the word in the air and on paper and/or on sand until each word is mastered. Once visualization is learned, spelling is no longer a problem in most cases.

Another challenging area for 2e students is math facts. Making math charts and looking for patterns is a very helpful intervention for these students. Math anxiety is prevalent among these students. Edward's story in this book personifies the student who knows the math concepts but can't get them down on paper. Mr. Delman's, M. Ed., method for helping his students calm down before a math test is also shared in this book and should be very helpful.

Twice exceptional students can be hyperactive at times and can also have periods of deep concentration. In many cases the hyperactivity can be caused by attention-deficit/hyperactivity disorder (ADHD). Allowing students to move around quietly in the back of the room without disturbing the other students is a very effective way of addressing this matter. Here, too, we often hear the same reframe, "But it isn't fair to the other students," to which the response is "But the other students aren't hyperactive."

In most cases it doesn't take long for the student to settle down and resume his/her work. Their periods of deep concentration are often focused on their passions and talents. They should be able to pursue these passions both at home and at school.

If a 2e student goes into a period of spaciness and has a glazed look, he/she can usually be brought back to the task at hand with a gentle tap on the shoulder. In addition, following directions can be difficult for 2e students. Parents and teachers should be sure to make eye contact with these individuals before giving any directions. Teachers should also write the directions on the board and possibly on paper as well.

Note taking can also be a problem for some twice exceptional students. They find using a computer or tablet very helpful. A "study buddy" of sharing notes has proved to be very helpful as well.

Not every 2e child will experience all the challenges discussed above but identifying those that are relevant will help your child/student achieve academic success. It will enable you to create a nurturing learning environment at home and in the classroom. Individual differences should be valued as a positive attribute.

Intervention will depend on the resources available in the school, in the school district, and time and personnel available in the classroom (see table 3.1). Volunteer tutors do a tremendous job with lessons developed by the classroom teachers. There are a number of excellent tutoring services that work with students individually or in small groups.

Some students only require intervention for a short period of time to remediate specific skills and to learn to compensate for their specific learning disability. Other students work with a tutor for years to remediate ongoing challenges presented by their specific learning disability and to address their giftedness and talents.

Intervention for the gifted exceptionality of twice exceptional students includes addressing the following:

- Learn quickly
- Excellent memories and retention of information
- Large vocabularies
- Complex sentence structure
- Enjoy problem-solving involving numbers and puzzles
- Long attention span
- Intense emotions, feelings, and reactions
- Abstract and insightful thinking
- Both complex and logical thinking
- Idealistic
- Concerned about social justice
- Persistent
- Intense concentration
- Ask probing questions
- Wide range of interests or a passion: extremely interested in only one area
- Divergent thinking
- Talents in specific domains such as art, music, writing, math, technology

These students should qualify for the Gifted and Talented programs in their schools in spite of their learning disabilities. But their learning capacities should also be taken into consideration in their regular class-rooms. For example, if they can learn a math concept by practicing it five times, they should not be forced to practice it the twenty times it takes for the average student to master the concept.

Table 3.1   Intervention for the Gifted Exceptionality of Twice Exceptional Students

Should be addressed in a Gifted/Talented Program	
GIFTEDNESS/TALENT	INTERVENTION
Learn quickly	Less practice items/allow to work at own pace
Excellent memories and retention of information	Provide challenging material
Large vocabularies	Major projects based on aptitudes
Complex sentence structure	Independent study/newspaper/year-book
Enjoy problem-solving involving numbers and puzzles	Provide opportunities to do them
Long attention span	Major projects
Intense emotions, feelings, and reactions	Drama/tutor
Abstract and insightful thinking	Debate team/newspaper/yearbook
Both complex and logical thinking	Debate team/newspaper/yearbook
Idealistic	Use foresight aptitude
Concerned about social justice	Community service projects/book group
Persistent	Long range project based on aptitudes
Intense concentration	Major projects based on Howard Gardner's Intelligences
Ask probing questions	Debate team
Wide range of interests or a passion: extremely interested in only one area	Projects in the appropriate areas
Divergent thinking	Debate team/tutor
Talents in specific domains such as art, music, writing, math, and technology	Projects in the appropriate areas

They should have a book at their Independent Reading Level at their desk that they can read when they finish class assignments more quickly than the rest of the class. Some gifted students are tutors for students in other classes or even their own. They might have projects in the area of social justice that they can work on while the rest of the class is completing an assignment. It is imperative to address their gifted exceptionality throughout the school day and at home as well.

Pat Antonopoulos, a kindergarten teacher in a suburban school district, did an Independent Research Project through the Education Department of the University of Missouri-Kansas City with the author to develop a classroom program to meet the needs of twice exceptional students. Although her program was conducted in her kindergarten classes, it can be used in all elementary grades. She named the program "The Center Approach" to meet the diverse needs of 46 children ranging in chronological age from 5.1 years to 6.2 years and an IQ range of 82–164. The morning section of the kindergarten had twenty-four students and the afternoon session had twenty-two students.

Each center had activities that encouraged creativity for all developmental levels. The centers also encouraged logical thinking, information processing, and detail recall. Many of the activities were verbal, easily accomplished with few materials, and exciting for the children.

Centers, also known as Learning Centers, give the teachers the opportunity to teach to the students' strengths and aptitudes. There is an in-depth discussion of student aptitudes in chapter 6. It also gives the students an opportunity to make choices. Learning Centers can be designed for individual work or group activities.

Every classroom should have a Literacy Center where students can curl up with a book. It is a place where they practice their writing skills at all levels. An Art Center will give students the opportunity to develop their creative aptitude. A Drama Center would have dress up clothes and give students another opportunity to develop their creative aptitude.

A Science Center will enable students with spatial thinking aptitude the opportunity to develop their gifts and talents in that area. Almost all classrooms have computers and many schools have Computer Labs.

Some children tend to favor one center. If that is the case, teacher guidance usually encourages the student to try other centers as well. Incorporation of Learning Centers varies from classroom to classroom depending on the teacher's approach to teaching.

Recognition of these differences was addressed by Mr. Les Short, an outstanding principal in the Park Hill School District. He hired three teachers for each grade level, one who taught with a structured style for students who learned best that way, a second teacher who taught in a classroom where students were given the opportunity to make quite a few choices, and a third who combined both methods.

He knew every child in his school and each year matched each child with the appropriate teacher. He also matched student-teachers accordingly which made student teaching for Park University Education majors a very positive experience.

The Learning Centers allow each student to function at his/her ability level. At the end of the school year, each student thought that he/she was Mrs. Antonopoulos' favorite student and most importantly, each child felt successful. Her work was cutting edge some twenty years ago but has proven to help all students, at all grade levels, especially special needs students including twice exceptional students achieve success over these many years.

CHAPTER 3. EARLY INTERVENTION

Post

EDUCATORS

1. What additional interventions do you plan to add to the original ones you planned to use?

2. What additions might you make to the learning environment you plan to create in your classroom?

3. Outline any additional types of interventions you plan to use for your gifted/talented students.

4. Outline any additional types of interventions you plan to accommodate the needs of your students who have learning disabilities.

PARENTS

1. Describe how you plan to advocate for your child's interventions.

2. What do you plan to do to support the interventions your child is receiving?

Chapter 4

Informal Reading Inventory

INTRODUCTION

EDUCATORS

1. Discuss how you plan to implement the results of the Informal Reading Inventories you administer.

2. Describe the type of intervention you will provide for those students scoring above grade level.

3. Describe the type of intervention you will provide for those students scoring below grade level.

PARENTS

1. Describe the type of advocacy you will provide on behalf of your child based on the results of the IRI.

As Professor Johnson approached the school entrance to supervise the seniors in her "Diagnosis and Remediation of Reading Problems" class she noticed a gentleman in coat and tie scrubbing down the stoop leading to the front door. She assumed someone had gotten ill there.

As she entered the building, she was met by the principal who told her when the first teacher arrived that morning, she found the body of a seventeen-year-old boy who had obviously tried to escape his adversary by seeking sanctuary in the school.

During the class meeting before they started their tutoring sessions, Professor Johnson advised her students to let their students talk about what had happened that morning for as long as they felt the need to do so and not to force the tutoring if they wanted the time to talk. The tutors proceeded to the all-purpose room set up with pairs of portable desks to meet with their respective students.

At their regular half-hour post-tutoring sharing session every single senior reported that they were able to conduct their planned tutoring session. None of their students felt the need to talk about the murder scene or the victim. Professor Johnson always stopped at the principal's office before she left the school.

On that day she reported what her students had told her had transpired in their sessions. The principal said,

> Your students and my teachers were the only ones who were traumatized by this tragedy. Research shows that in low-income neighborhoods like this one, almost every child experiences gun violence before the age of five. It is simply a fact of life for them. Many children don't want to go home at the end of the day. They feel safer here. They receive two warm meals, breakfast and lunch as well as the help from caring adults.

You will meet Emma, one of the students tutored in this low-income school later in this chapter. Emma was the beneficiary of a university's student field experience.

In order for classroom teachers to meet the special needs of their twice exceptional students, they must understand that they can, in fact, screen for certain difficulties experienced by students who would otherwise "fall through the cracks." One of the most valuable diagnostic tools available to classroom teachers is the IRI.

The idea of the IRI came to Professor Thorndike in the 1920s. He was considered by some to be the "father of educational psychology" at that time. It evolved as his concern grew over what he considered to be a lack of attention to students' individual differences by schools. Thorndike maintained that at least 40 percent of students were expected to read material that was too difficult for them.

Thus, he established criteria for reading levels. Also, a key component was the concept of being able to "observe student reading behavior." Today, many refer to that as the ability to "observe the student during the process of reading."

It has been a century since Professor Thorndike conceived of the idea of the Informal Reading Inventory and during that time it has undergone many changes in line with the changes taking place in reading instruction. It evolved to become a diagnostic tool for teachers with many different approaches as many programs continued to change their instructional formats.

Professor Nicolas Silvaroli published his first *Classroom Reading Inventory* (CRI) in 1965 using the Subskills format. This was followed by five additional editions using the Subskills format. In his Seventh Edition he added a Literature format. He designed the CRI to enable teachers to identify a pattern in word recognition and/or comprehension development.

The Twelfth Edition of the *CRI* was published by Warren H. Wheelock and Connie J. Campbell in 2012 after the death of Nicolas Silvaroli. They added multicultural stories and themes, global themes, and high-interest topics to the reading passages.

They also included online and adult testing material that remained online until the death of Warren Wheelock.

The latest edition also includes updated word lists, correction of ambiguous items, and improved formatting. These changes and additions were based on feedback from CRI users. Professor Wheelock told his students that he often used older editions of the CRI because then he could be sure that the students had not read the paragraphs previously.

The CRI is an IRI to be administered by the classroom teacher in the classroom. Its name in contrast to other Informal Reading Inventories underscores its importance for use by the classroom teacher in the classroom setting while other students are working independently. The short period of time it takes to administer and the ease of administration make it a vital instrument for teachers to use.

It enables teachers to *observe* the student in the *process* of reading and to establish his/her Independent, Instructional, Frustration, and

Listening Capacity reading levels. It is a diagnostic tool to enable teachers to identify twice exceptional as well as other special needs students.

One of the strengths of the CRI is that it enables the classroom teacher to observe consistent errors in both word recognition and comprehension. It also gives the teacher quantitative as well as qualitative insight into the student's reading ability. That is why the teacher's knowledge and understanding of the reading process is so important.

The classroom teacher is able to assess whether the student is having more difficulty with word recognition or comprehension skills or equal difficulty with both. The classroom teacher is able to assess whether word recognition skills differ with consonants, vowels, or syllables. Are comprehension skills problems with factual, inferential, or vocabulary material?

Is the student a "word caller," a student who can decode fluently, but not take meaning from the words? In other words, he/she is not "thinking with the print." During the intake interview at the University of Missouri-Kansas City one mother explained that she was enrolling her third-grade daughter for reading remediation because her teacher had discovered that she had no comprehension of the material she was decoding.

Because she read so fluently neither her parents nor her previous teachers had noticed that she was not comprehending as she was decoding. She is an example of the high percentage of Reading Clinic students who are remediated by simply reteaching basic reading comprehension skills.

Classroom teachers are also urged to observe whether students have physical issues such as problems with eyesight or a hearing deficit causing a delay in normal reading acquisition. As reading problems continue, anxiety often causes additional problems as might an undiagnosed learning disability.

Many 2e students report that they know "deep down" that they are as smart or smarter than their classmates who are reading at grade level and can't understand why they aren't able to read as well. This also causes anxiety, which is often a key roadblock in reading remediation.

Background knowledge is very important in reading comprehension. The more an individual knows about a topic the more he/she will learn from new information on that topic. Comprehension takes place by relating new material in a text to background knowledge. Language development is another important factor of reading acquisition.

For example: The inner-city mother wanting her preschool child to get his sneakers from the closet might point to the closet and say "Go get your sneakers!" The middle-class mother would say "Tommy, please go to the closet and bring me your sneakers. I'll help you put them on so we can go to the playground."

The enormous difference in language development that the two children bring with them as they start school has been well documented. Many Teacher Education Programs are addressing these differences to prepare teachers to meet the special needs and deficits of inner-city children.

The CRI is only as effective as the individual who is administering it. Again, the individual must have a strong knowledge base and understanding of the reading process. With a solid understanding of reading that individual is able to observe the student in the process of reading and to establish the reading levels for each student with diverse learning needs.

The CRI can be administered in twelve to fifteen minutes by an experienced teacher. However, it does take practice, between five and ten administrations before an individual can expect to administer the CRI in that period of time. The reading levels established by the inventory include the Independent Level, Instructional Level, Frustration Level, and Listening Capacity Level (see figures 4.1).

The Independent Level is the level at which the student can read with ease and without teacher's assistance, 99 percent of word recognition accuracy and 90 percent of comprehension accuracy.

The best way to improve reading skills is to *read, read, read.* All students should have a book at their desks at their Independent Level to read for pleasure.

All teachers should provide time for such independent reading. This form of reading "practice" shows students that reading can be an enjoyable experience in school as well as a learning experience. A fifteen-minute period of independent reading can give the classroom teacher time to administer a CRI to a student in need of that assessment.

Reading books of their own choice with ease in the classroom helps to prepare students to be life-long learners. Reading is a skill and like any other skill, baseball, ballet, Olympic swimming, the more it is practiced the more proficient the individual becomes at it. Thus, the more the students read at their Independent Level the more proficient they become, the more they enjoy reading, the more they read and then the better they become at this very important skill.

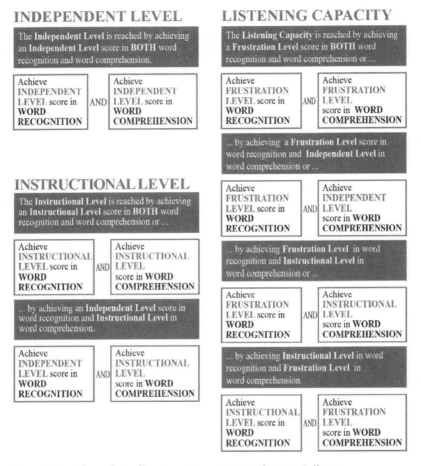

Figure 4.1   Informal Reading Inventory. *Source: Christina Sullivan.*

Unfortunately, students who are experiencing difficulties learning to read don't enjoy reading and don't practice it enough. Therefore, it is very important to establish their independent reading level and provide them with High-Interest/Low-Vocabulary books to practice reading and enjoy it.

Reading instruction should take place at the student's Instructional Level. That is 95 percent accuracy in word recognition and comprehension of at least 75 percent of the material read. Anything below these scores is measured as the Frustration Level and student should *not* be put in the position of trying to function at the Frustration Level.

An important tool available to teachers, enabling them to identify diverse learners, is the Listening Capacity of the IRI. Once the student has reached the Frustration Level, the teacher reads to the student as long as the student can answer comprehension questions with 60–75 percent accuracy. The highest level achieved is scored as the student's Listening Capacity Level.

For many twice exceptional students, their Listening Capacity is many levels above their Frustration Level and above their grade level. *This is a key indicator of twice exceptionality.*

Their exceptional intelligence enables them to comprehend at a level well above their grade level but their disability, whatever it might be, delays their Instructional Level. This is what makes the IRI such an important diagnostic tool (see figure 4.2).

Reading Levels

The following reading levels should be established for each student:

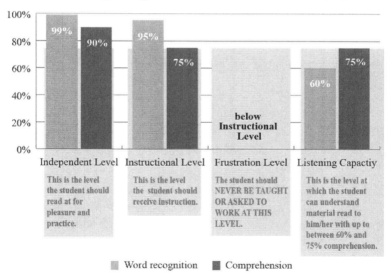

Figure 4.2 Classroom Reading Inventory: Reading Levels. *Source: Christina Sullivan.*

For example, Emma, a twice exceptional student who is in the third grade, is at the Instructional Level at the first grade with an Independent

Level score of primer. Her scores indicate that she is two years behind in reading instruction. Her Listening Capacity Level is at the sixth-grade level. Her reading difficulty has masked her giftedness and her giftedness has masked her reading disability.

Once her reading levels were established, her university tutor and her classroom tutor were able to deliver instruction to assure success. Emma was able to read High-Interest/Low-Vocabulary books at her Independent Level to practice, practice, practice this skill and she received instruction at her Instructional Level.

Her teacher also provided audiobooks and online books in "The Office," a quiet corner of the classroom for students to go to do special work.

Thus, Emma's giftedness was addressed by being able to listen to audiobooks at her intellectual level and her learning disability was addressed by intervention at the proper Instructional Level.

The Listening Capacity score is a key to identifying students like Emma, and with practice this can be done in twelve to fifteen minutes. In this case, the university tutor administered the CRI. It was a valuable lesson for her to be able to identify 2e students. In addition to the scores, the tutor learned quite a bit by observing the student in the process of reading. She shared this with her classmates and professor in the post-tutoring session as well as with Emma's classroom teacher in the report she wrote as part of the course requirements.

When the students are placed at their correct reading levels they often can gain as much as three to four grade levels in a matter of months. This is often the case in the Reading Clinic.

Seniors at Park University are required to take a six-hour course in "The Diagnosis and Remediation of Reading Difficulties in the Classroom" in the classroom. They spend three hours twice a week for fourteen weeks in a school setting where the university students work one-on-one with four students for at least half an hour each. Six of the thirty students who were referred by their classroom teachers for reading remediation were identified by their college tutors as being "twice exceptional" based on the establishment of their respective Listening Capacities as far above grade level. Thus, these students received both remediation and enrichment, which proved to be enormously successful. Post-testing and teacher observations validated the students' success each semester.

It is hoped that with the increased understanding of the importance and value of the Listening Capacity score in the CRI, more teachers will turn to this instrument to identify twice exceptional and special needs students. If a student has a behavior problem in class, it only takes fifteen minutes to assess whether twice exceptionality or other special needs are causing frustration and acting out.

Wheelock and Campbell point out that not only is the CRI a diagnostic tool but that it will improve teaching because it will "align your instruction more clearly and precisely with the reading needs, levels, skills and comprehension priorities of your students."

The purpose of the Spelling Survey is to gather additional information about a student's ability to integrate and express letterform, letter-sound relationships. However, many students who experience reading delays also experience spelling problems. So much so, the next chapter is devoted entirely to this topic.

CHAPTER 4. INFORMAL READING INVENTORY

Post

EDUCATORS

1. Discuss any additional plans you might add to your original plan to implement the results of the Informal Reading Inventories you administer.

2. Describe any additional types of intervention you will provide for those students scoring above grade level.

3. Describe any additional types of intervention you will provide for those students scoring below grade level.

PARENTS

1. Describe any additional types of advocacies you will provide on behalf of your child based on the results of the Informal Reading Inventory.

Chapter 5

Stopwatch Spelling

INTRODUCTION

EDUCATORS

1. Relate Stopwatch Spelling to your reading program.

2. Relate Stopwatch Spelling to your curriculum.

PARENTS

1. Relate Stopwatch Spelling to your child's homework assignments.

Troy's mother enrolled him in the Reading Clinic at the University of Missouri-Kansas City because he was in the seventh grade but reading at the fourth-grade level. His parents are both teachers and he is the fourth child with six siblings. None of his siblings were experiencing any learning challenges.

Troy had a documented hearing loss and had preferential seating next to the teacher's desk in the front row. His teacher reported that when she was explaining things, Troy sometimes got a blank expression on his face and she thought he might be developmentally delayed.

The tutors in the Reading Clinic are Master's Level and Doctoral students fulfilling the field components of advanced courses in "Diagnosis and Remediation of Reading Problems in the Classroom." As such, they administer instruments that they will use in their classrooms.

Troy's tutor's name was Sally and they really "hit it off" very quickly. The first instrument she administered was a "Test of Letter Knowledge" and discovered that Troy could not differentiate between the letter *g* and *j*, probably because of his hearing loss. Sally retaught the letters *g* and *j* and once mastered Troy quickly was able to close the grade-level gap. By the end of the academic year, he was reading at grade level.

Professor John Sherk reported that 80–85 percent of the students in the Reading Clinic show improvement in their reading performance as a result of being retaught basic reading skills.

Troy certainly was one of those students.

One of the instruments administered by students enrolled in a graduate level course on intelligence testing is the WISC, Wechsler Intelligence Scale for Children. It is an individually administered test for children between the ages of 6 and 16. Troy scored in the Superior range and the subtest scores indicated that he was twice exceptional. Thus, his gifted range intelligence explained why he was able to catch up to grade-level reading so quickly.

Important lesson: Students must have mastery of every letter of the alphabet before they can learn to read. The author shared Troy's story with her classes to make that point. One of her student administered the "Test of Letter Knowledge" to her son who was in high school and still struggling with reading. She discovered that there were several letters that he did not know, retaught them, and successfully remediated his reading problem. Obviously, everyone had just assumed by the time her son was in high school he knew all the letters.

Another important lesson learned from Troy is that we cannot make assumptions and must check for the most basic elements that are part of the reading process. Students with diverse learning needs often miss these basic elements and must have them retaught in order to master the reading process.

When Troy was well on his way to experiencing success in reading, he came to a tutoring session really downcast. He had spent two hours on his spelling lesson and still failed the weekly spelling test. Knowing that his mind worked very quickly, his tutor thought the speed in "Stopwatch Spelling" might really appeal to him and she considered the possibility that he might require the reteaching of visualization.

Learning to spell is a complex and multifaceted task. It is influenced by the student's cognitive ability, appropriate instruction, level of language knowledge and usage, interest in material, visual and auditory perception, imagery, visualization, long and short term memory, learning style, attitude, motivation: (see figure 5.1).

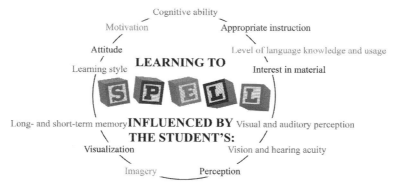

Figure 5.1   Learning to Spell. *Source: Christina Sullivan.*

Teachers/tutors should use the *Check List* in the Appendix as they prepare the list of spelling words to teach the 2e student. Most important is to be sure to have the list at the student's instructional level based on the Informal Reading Inventory.

Considerable research has established a close relationship between a student's reading problems and tendency toward spelling delays. In order for children to become developmental readers and spellers they must first understand sound-symbol relationships, the ability to visualize, and be able to "hold the whole word in mind while simultaneously attending to parts within the word."

The ability to "hold words still in their minds" while they learn to spell them is a specific skill that has been used to describe visualization in a spelling context. Visualization is a skill that is not automatically attained by children and must be taught and retaught until mastered. This is especially important for students who are experiencing difficulty learning to spell.

"Stopwatch Spelling" was developed as an individualized approach to teach a specific skill, visualization, to disabled readers/spellers who were making progress in reading but continued to experience difficulty with spelling. The focus of this strategy is to teach students *how to* "hold words in their minds" and visualize them while learning to spell.

Although most current spelling programs teach the skill of visualization as part of the instructional process, it appears that the skill is not retaught often enough and "how to" visualize is not taught adequately to meet the needs of some disabled readers/spellers. In many cases, the lack of the ability to visualize is the key to the spelling problem.

Although "Stopwatch Spelling" was developed as an individualized approach to spelling instruction it could also be characterized as eclectic. Because spelling is essentially a visual task, "Stopwatch Spelling" stresses the visual aspect of spelling instruction; however, learning to spell requires some auditory and kinesthetic skills as well as a great deal of practice. Therefore, this strategy includes oral reading, visual memory, auditory, motor, and graphic associations.

"Stopwatch Spelling" can be used in the classroom by the teacher, peer tutors, volunteer tutors, and as part of a cooperative learning program. It can also be used effectively by parents at home.

The first step in the spelling session is the administration of the *Pretest*. The lesson should consist of ten words, graded to be consistent with the student's instructional reading level.

The student then *reads* the spelling list to the teacher/tutor. They should then discuss the words to ascertain the student's understanding of the word meaning. Discussion continues until the student is able to read the list fluently and it is clear that the student knows the meaning of the word. Note any words that could not be read fluently.

Student then *copies* list of words missed on the pretest from printed spelling list onto the *Focus Time Sheet*. The teacher/tutor will then use the Focus Time Sheet to record the period of time it takes for the student to focus on each spelling word.

Teacher/tutor explains "Stopwatch Spelling" to the student as follows:

> Pretend that your brain is a camera and that you are going to take a picture of the first word on your spelling list. Tell me when you start to focus on that word, and I will time how long it takes for you to be able to look at the word until you close your eyes and start to spell the word aloud to me. I will then record your time next to the word on the list you copied.

If the student cannot spell the word correctly after the first focus he/she repeats the focus procedure, and a second focus time is added to the original time recorded. Students quickly learn that it is better to focus a little longer the first time if necessary.

The student then writes the word on the practice sheet and checks the word against the list. If it is correct, teacher/tutor covers the word and asks the student to write the word once more. The word is learned when the student writes the word correctly twice. If the word is not spelled correctly, repeat focus procedure until each word is learned.

This procedure is followed until each spelling word on the list of missed words is learned. The procedure enables the student to learn one word at a time until the entire list is learned.

An oral or written review should take place after each five words.

A *post-test* should be given on the entire spelling lesson administered on the pretest.

For most students, practice writing the spelling words twice after focusing on the word is sufficient to learn each word. Research has shown that asking students to write spelling words five or ten times is counterproductive. After two or three times the students no longer are concentrating on the process and just writing the words by rote.

Troy's first session using "Stopwatch Spelling" is found on the following pages (see figures 5.2, 5.3, 5.4, and 5.5). It should be noted that instead of taking two hours, Troy learned his spelling words in less than two minutes, 100.62 seconds to be precise. Instead of being a frustrating exercise each week spelling was a routine class, no longer a disability.

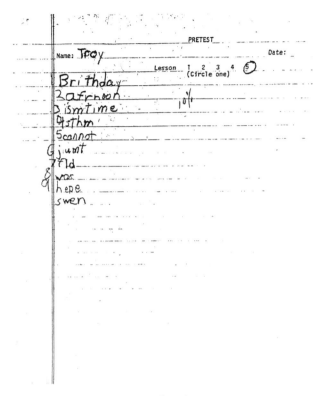

Figure 5.2   Pretest. *Source: Courtesy of student.*

Once again, we see how identification of a very specific problem and appropriate intervention enables a twice exceptional student to achieve success in the classroom.

Troy's story reflects not only 2e students' experience with spelling but also that of many other students who are nontraditional learners. It underscores the need to identify the skills that must be retaught and how successful reteaching is. His story should give teachers/tutors a better understanding of the complex nature of spelling, the importance

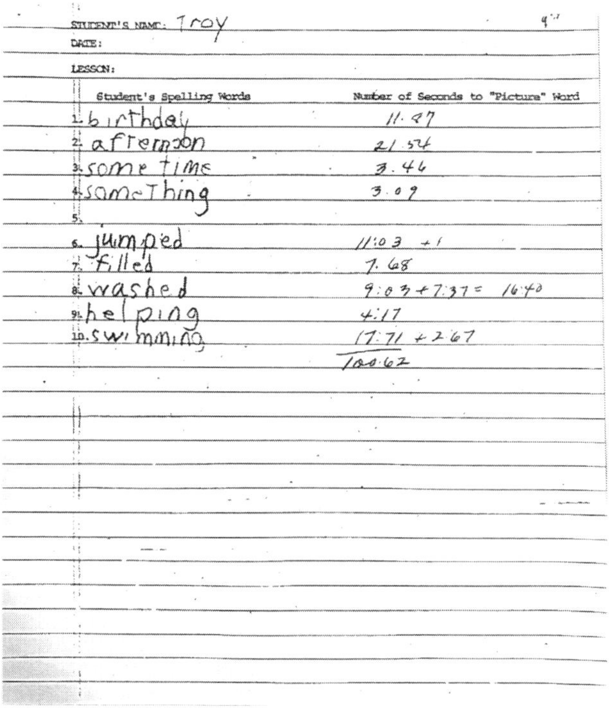

STUDENT'S NAME: Troy

DATE:

LESSON:

Student's Spelling Words	Number of Seconds to "Picture" Word
1. birthday	11.47
2. afternoon	21.54
3. some time	3.46
4. someThing	3.09
5.	
6. jumped	11:03 +1
7. filled	7.68
8. washed	9:03 + 7:37 = 16:40
9. helping	4:17
10. swimming	17:71 + 2:67
	100.62

Figure 5.3 Focus Time Sheet. *Source*: *Courtesy of student.*

of visualization, and a specific strategy, "Stopwatch Spelling," to teach and reteach that skill.

Troy's score of 100 ever in spelling gave him new confidence that spilled over to all his other subjects. He moved from failure and frustration to an understanding that he had the ability to succeed academically. It also improved his relationship with his siblings, and he stayed in touch with his tutor, Sally, through college and into adulthood. This student, who one teacher thought might be developmentally delayed, graduated with a degree in engineering!

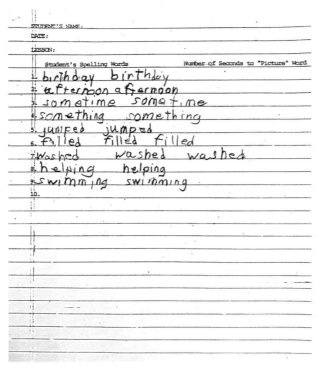

Figure 5.4   Practice Sheet. *Source: Courtesy of student.*

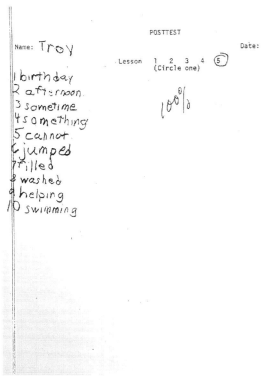

POSTTEST

Name: Troy

Date:

Lesson 1 2 3 4 ⑤
(Circle one)

100%

1 birthday
2 afternoon.
3 sometime
4 something
5 cannot.
6 jumped
7 filled
8 washed
9 helping
10 swimming

Figure 5.5 Post-Test. *Source: Courtesy of student.*

CHAPTER 5. STOPWATCH SPELLING

Post

EDUCATORS

1. Discuss how Stopwatch Spelling relates to your reading program.

2. Discuss how Stopwatch Spelling relates to your curriculum.

PARENTS

1. How has Stopwatch Spelling helped your child's spelling homework assignments?

Chapter 6

Twice Exceptional Students
Natural Aptitudes

INTRODUCTION

EDUCATORS

1. Discuss how you will identify the natural abilities of each of your students.

2. Discuss how you will implement what you learn about each student's natural abilities in your classroom.

PARENTS

1. Describe your child's natural abilities.

2. How did you identify them?

3. Discuss the importance of your child's natural abilities in his/her everyday life.

Tim was at his doctor's office for his annual check-up before the beginning of the new school year. Doctor Bancroft said, "Tim, I guess you're headed for another straight A year." To which Tim replied, "Actually not since I can get Cs without doing any work."

Tim's mom and Doctor Bancroft looked at each other in surprise and both were concerned by Tim's flippant response. Tim was a good student, well-liked by his peers, and a whiz at technology.

"Tim, you aren't serious, are you?" his mom asked. Tim just shrugged his shoulders and headed for the door.

Several weeks later, shortly after the start of the school year, Tim's mom received a phone call from his teacher reporting that the regular fall semester testing indicated that Tim had scored at sixth grade in math at the beginning of the eighth grade.

"How can that be?" Alarmed, she asked. "He does such advanced work with computers."

"I don't know," his teacher replied. "You might consider having Tim receive an educational evaluation."

Given the episode in the doctor's office and this startling report, she decided this was a good idea and did have Tim receive an educational evaluation. The evaluation documented that Tim was twice exceptional and that his giftedness had masked the fact that he had a learning disability and his learning disability masked giftedness.

He was tutored in math and with his superior intelligence he quickly caught up to grade level. But well into the semester, he fell behind again. His parents hired a tutor once more and after a few sessions, the tutor said to his parents, "I can't continue to take your money. Tim learns the 40 minutes class lesson in 20 minutes!"

When his parents asked Tim why he could do so well with his tutor and yet not learn the material in class, Tim replied, "At the beginning of class the white board is empty and by the end of the period it is full and I don't know how all the writing got there."

It was clear that he had one of the characteristics of twice exceptional children, a mind that works very quickly and then wanders. Having identified this problem, Tim tried his best to stay focused but before he left for college his parents had him tested by the Johnson O'Connor Research Foundation.

Johnson O'Connor developed an aptitude test that he administered to his employees at General Electric. He had discovered that employees were more productive and happy employees when they worked in areas that used their natural aptitudes. Friends and relatives were so impressed by this test that they asked if they too could be tested. That prompted the opening of the first Johnson O'Connor Research Foundation in Boston in 1922.

Johnson O'Connor believed that every individual has natural talents that should be nurtured and used. He urged people "to choose careers that fit to how their minds work naturally." He also maintained that "the individual who knows his own aptitudes and their relative strengths chooses more intelligently among the world's host of opportunities."

Aptitudes are natural talents for doing certain kinds of things *quickly and easily*. They are talents you are born with such as musical and artistic. Aptitude testing will identify natural abilities. There are no right and wrong answers, only how the individual scores in one test compared to another.

Tasks such as remembering designs, assembling blocks, listening to tunes all are an objective measurements of how *naturally, easily, and quickly* the task is accomplished by the individual. It is not influenced by past experience or educational background. These tests do not test feelings or interests.

The importance of the information that these tests provide for students, their parents, and teachers again is about their *natural abilities, patterns, strengths, and weaknesses*. The Aptitude Teacher Observation Form (see table 6.1) should help the classroom teacher note those learning tasks that his/her students learn *quickly and easily*. This should be very helpful for teachers to teach to the strengths of 2e and 3e students as well as all special needs students in the classrooms.

The results of Tim's testing sessions underscored how quickly his mind works. The clinician told Tim he was going to speak very quickly during the report session in order to be sure to keep his attention.

He also recommended that Tim record his college lectures and classes on a high-speed recorder so that he could play them back quickly. This proved to be enormously helpful and successful. It eliminated much of the problems that had plagued him throughout his earlier school years.

The following is a list of aptitudes (see table 6.2) developed over the last ninety-nine years by the Johnson O'Connor Research Foundation, some actually going back to 1922 and the work of Johnson O'Connor himself. These relate to 2e and 3e students who are fourteen years and older. The aptitudes are innate and stable.

Structural Visualization measures spatial thinking, thinking in 3D. These individuals like to take things apart and put them together again. Like to figure out how things work. Albert Einstein, Thomas Edison, and Nikola Tesla all described their creative process as including visualization. A study of Einstein's brain showed that the lobe linked to spatial thinking was 15 percent larger than the average.

Table 6.1   Aptitude Teacher Observation Form

Name:			Date:
Subject	*Naturally*	*Easily*	*Quickly*
Social Studies			
Language Arts			
Science			
Science Lab			
Math			
Computers			
Art			
Music			
Independent Study			
Physical Education			
Other			

Ideaphonia measures the rate of the flow of ideas — free-flowing, spontaneous, nonlinear, divergent thinking. Johnson O'Connor recommends that students who score high in this area have the opportunity to do a lot of writing, work on the school newspaper, yearbook, blogging

Table 6.2   Johnson O'Connor Research Foundation Aptitude List: Grades 1–8

Name:		Grade:	Date:
	Naturally	*Easily*	*Quickly*
Structural Visualization—3D			
Flow of Ideas			
Foresight			
Inductive Research			
Analytical Reasoning			
Number Facility			
Auditory			
Visual			
Verbal Communication			
Perceptual Speed and Accuracy			
Dexterity			
Grip-hand Strength			
Approach to Work			
Vocabulary*			
Interests*			

*Not aptitudes, but important in the application of aptitudes.

theater, student council, tutor, brainstorming all areas where the flow of ideas is put to good use.

Foresight measures the "ability to see possibilities where none exist." The aptitude of foresight allows the student to set long-term goals. It is the ability to imagine what could exist — predicts potential. These students are creative and should be given the opportunity to be creative in their assignments that are linked to idea generation and creativity.

Inductive Reasoning is the ability to diagnose, problem-solve, make connections with research, "ability to connect the dots." They are able to move quickly through the material presented to them. Johnson O'Connor is quoted as saying that "Inductive Reasoning is the ability to sense a unifying principle running miscellany." Individuals who score high are both accurate and fast, critical thinkers and divergent thinkers. They are individuals who analyze and/or synthesize the problem before coming to a solution.

Analytical Reasoning is the aptitude that allows students to plan and organize the systems efficiently and apply executive skills. Activities such as scrapbooking, genealogy, puzzles, tutoring are all activities recommended for these students. For students who are low in this aptitude, starting projects early is highly encouraged to give them plenty of time to get organized.

Numerical Aptitude is the ability to find trends or patterns in numbers. It is a number facility, remembering groups of numbers naturally, quickly, and accurately. This natural aptitude is easy to identify and should be nurtured. It is also connected to general reasoning. Analyzing, interpreting, or reasoning is done with numerical information.

We often hear about just the opposite of this aptitude among students who experience a great deal of math anxiety and fear — math phobia. It is suggested that this might go back to the way math was introduced and taught initially.

Auditory Aptitude is among the first aptitudes to be isolated. It has been part of the battery of tests since the 1930s. Many researchers connect this with artistic talent. Individuals with this aptitude learn languages easily. The auditory aptitude is used in many diverse professions. For example, the cardiologist listening to the heartbeat, any doctor for that matter!

Visual Aptitude is considered to be an "observational learning style." This is usually pretty obvious to parents, teachers, and the students themselves. They gravitate to art and design, puzzles and photography.

Silograms is the aptitude that is high in verbal communication. Students with this aptitude enjoy writing and editing, crossword puzzles and word games like Scrabble and the popular online game of Words with Friends. They should be encouraged to keep journals. Flashcards are good study aids for these students. Silograms is this aptitude author's name in reverse, Margolis!

Graphoria hands-on learners. Students have fine motor skills and attend to details. They should be encouraged to share their note-taking skills with 2e and 3e students who find note-taking very challenging. As a group, women average higher scores than men on Graphoria tests.

Dexterity Aptitude also measures fine motor skills. They benefit from an experiential approach to learning. This was the first test actually isolated by Johnson O'Connor himself for the selection of workers for the assembly line. He found workers who scored high on the Dexterity Aptitude test were successful on the assembly and, in addition, that they enjoyed their jobs.

Grip measures hand strength. These students require a lot of movement and frequent breaks. They benefit from project-based learning. They do well with outdoor activities, independent studies, and apprenticeship programs.

Workplace Personality measures how the individual actually approaches his/her job and the workplace.

Vocabulary is not an aptitude but is tested in this battery because Johnson O'Connor considered words to be "tools of thought," a communication tool. The test is a measure of general word knowledge.

"An extensive knowledge of the exact meanings of English words accompanies outstanding success in this country. More often than any other single characteristic which the Johnson O'Connor Research Foundation has been able to isolate."

The same is true of the results of the Wechsler Intelligence Tests. The high score in the Vocabulary subtest is the "single best indicator" of innate intelligence. Among Howard Gardner's Multiple Intelligences, Linguistic Intelligence is most used in school.

Interest, belief, and values are all considered to be important factors in how aptitudes play out. The overlap between aptitude and interest is considered to be the most ideal arrangement.

We have discussed how important the teacher's observation is to enable them to meet each student's academic needs. Teaching students' aptitudes is also very important. The *first Check List* is a guide for teacher observation of general course work and the second is an application of the types of Johnson O'Connor aptitudes as adjusted for younger students. Adapting a hundred years of research of natural abilities to younger students can be a tool for twice exceptional students to succeed.

CHAPTER 6. TWICE EXCEPTIONAL STUDENTS: NATURAL APTITUDES

Post

EDUCATORS

1. Discuss how you will identify the natural abilities of each of your students based on your reading of this chapter.

2. Discuss how you will implement what you learn about each student's natural abilities in your classroom.

3. What type of learning center might you set up to address your students' natural abilities?

PARENTS

1. Did you identify any additional natural abilities that your child has based on reading this chapter?

2. Discuss the importance of your child's natural abilities in his/her everyday life and the life of your family.

Chapter 7

Thrice Exceptional Students' Challenges

INTRODUCTION

EDUCATORS

1. Describe how you plan to address the needs of your thrice exceptional students.

2. Discuss the various types of thrice exceptional students.

3. Discuss how you plan to identify and intervene on behalf of your 2e and 3e students.

PARENTS

1. Discuss how you plan to advocate on behalf of your thrice exceptional child.

2. Describe the school environment you expect for your 3e child.

3. What specific needs do you expect to be met for your 3e child?

For many years, Bingham Junior High School was a college prep feeder school for Southwest High School. As the neighborhood changed, most students were no longer college prep and some were actually "at-risk students" who were reading far below grade level. Quite a few of these students skipped class and wandered through the Waldo stores, often shoplifting. Waldo is an old middle-class neighborhood in south Kansas City.

The Waldo merchants met and decided to pool some funds to see if the Reading Department at the University of Missouri Kansas City would develop a program to help the "at-risk students" improve their reading skills and hopefully keep them in class rather than in the Waldo stores.

Dr. John Sherk, a professor in the Reading Department, developed this program and recruited several doctoral students to participate in the project. Dr. Sherk held a meeting with the teachers of the classes from which the students would come. He carefully outlined the project to a clearly hostile group of teachers whose attitude was "how do you think you are going to succeed with these students if we aren't."

One teacher said, "I have always taught 8th graders *Animal Farm* and I am going to continue to teach *Animal Farm,* I don't care at what level the students are reading. What do you think you are going to accomplish coming here?"

Dr. Sherk replied quietly,

> We conduct these special workshops for students who are having difficulty acquiring reading skills at grade level. On average the students raise their reading levels a full two grade levels during the sixteen-week semester. We expect the same outcome here. That should make *Animal Farm* much more accessible for your students.

Each of the doctoral students and Dr. Sherk worked with a group of five students, two sessions per week for sixteen weeks. The average improvement for the thirty-plus seventh- and eighth-grade students in the program was two reading levels.

In conjunction with this project, a three-step process was designed: observation, evaluation, and intervention (see figure 7.1). The first step was teacher observation. Classroom teachers were asked to observe their students and select those they thought might most benefit from our program. Next, each student was evaluated to establish his or her instructional level. Then, intervention took place.

THREE-STEP PROCESS

Figure 7.1   Three-Step Process. *Source: Christina Sullivan.*

The average gain of two years in their reading levels was made possible because of the small group and each student was being taught at his/her instructional level. One student, Marge, started at the third-grade level and gained five grade levels, scoring at the eighth-grade level on her post-test. Marge was asked how she was able to accomplish that.

Marge responded,

> You showed me that I could improve my reading. I had given up on ever improving my reading skills. But each week I got better on the work I did with you. I realized I could learn, and I did. You showed me I could read better.

The team was so impressed with Marge's success that they followed up on her the following year in high school. They found that she was continuing to experience success and doing grade-level work. Marge is an excellent example of a thrice exceptional student. Clearly, she had neither been identified as a gifted student nor had her learning disability been diagnosed. Thus, she fell further and further behind.

Her gifted exceptionality allowed her to gain five grade levels in sixteen weeks. She was taught to compensate for her learning disability in the small group setting. Her third exceptionality was race — African American — which placed her in a school in which the teachers were teaching subject matter and not individual students. The teachers were not willing to recognize that Bingham Junior High School was no longer a college prep school.

It clearly lacked the leadership to require a change in curriculum to meet the academic needs of the student body. Had the race not been a third exceptionality for Marge, she probably would have been referred for an Educational Evaluation in second grade like some of the other students discussed were. So, neither her giftedness nor her learning disability was identified or addressed.

Carl Sabatino, Publisher, and Chris Wiebe, Ed.D. Managing Editor of Variations2e, have published a Summer 2021 edition that hopefully will make an enormous impact on the field of education. They have "given a voice to the scholars and educators whose important contributions and continuing work explore the intersections of race, culture, giftedness and twice exceptionality."

They have also given voice to the families of color, each one a story that must be heard and heeded. We must listen and become part of the solution. We have e, 2e, 3e, and might even consider 4e, gifted and talented, learning disabled, black and what comes all too often with black, and poverty (see figure 7.2).

According to a 2016 *The New York Times* article, white students are twice as likely to be identified for giftedness and/or twice exceptionality as black and Latino students. However, when nonverbal IQ tests were administered to Latino kids in Broward County, Florida, between 2005 and 2010 the percentage of those students identified as gifted *tripled*. This certainly sends a clear and compelling message and a call to action.

Many Latino students are the children of first-generation immigrants who have no idea what might be available for their thrice exceptional children nor how to navigate the system. There is another major concern for families who are not documented. Schools are not supposed to investigate whether students come from documented families. There is a great amount of fear of the severe consequences in many Latino communities.

Maria Gentry summarized the status of Indigenous youth in education as overlooked, underrepresented, and invisible and we have the statistics to support her assertion. American Indian Alaska Native (AIAN) youth are 8 percent less likely than all other race categories to even attend a school that identified youth and gift talents. Underrepresentation is a national problem.

The Indian Education Act (1972) and the Indian Self-Determination Act (1975) provided grants to provide supplemental programming to public schools with Indigenous students. Control of Bureau of Indian Affairs (BIA) was shifted to tribal governments, thus most of the reservation boarding schools were closed.

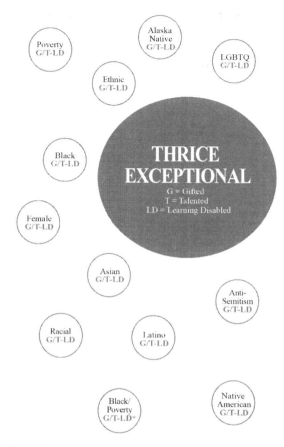

Figure 7.2 Thrice Exceptional. *Source: Christina Sullivan.*

As of this writing, there are 573 federally recognized AIAN native nations in thirty-five states. Ninety percent of their children attend public schools, 8 percent attend Bureau of Indian Education Schools.

AIAN students were 8 percent less likely than all other race categories to even attend a school that identifies students with gifts and talents. Students of color, including AIAN, are grossly underrepresented in Gifted and Talented Programs across the country. This is another call for action to address the third exceptionality for AIAN students.

Lara-Cooper (2014), who studied the Hupa, Yorok, and Karuk members living on the Hoopa Valley Indian Reservation (HVIR), wrote:

> *Giftedness can be defined through k'winya, 'nya:n-ma 'awhiniw ("the human way"), meaning to live in balance and harmony with the world by having honor and respect for community members, the environment, self, ancestors and creation. The human way is guided by language and culture and characterized by honor, humility, patience and gratitude, discipline, compassion, a good heart, generosity, responsibility, and respect; maintaining relationships with the human, natural, and spiritual realms; understanding and valuing the HVIR worldview; and making a contribution to HVIR community. (p. 6)*

This is a challenge addressed to educators to go beyond test scores and quantification of giftedness. The two steps involved are to examine the equity of the gifted program and to broaden the program to reflect the student body of the school. This challenge resonates throughout the thrice exceptional communities, indeed the 3e world.

Dr. Jaime Castellano is one of our nation's leading authorities in the education of Hispanic/Latino students and in identifying and serving low-income, racially, culturally, and linguistically diverse gifted students. He has developed a number of guiding principles to promote diversity, equity, and inclusion necessary to provide an appropriate education for 3e students.

There must be a *vision* established for the education of 2e and 3e students and *standards* identified as well. Progress must be evaluated to identify strengths and areas that need improvement. Teachers and administers must have the *skill, ability, and desire* to teach 2e and 3e students. Teachers, school administrators, and parents form a "web of support" for their 2e and 3e students.

Dr. Castellano maintains that classroom teachers and school administrators should receive training on identifying 2e and 3e students which is precisely the purpose of this book. He suggests that identification can occur at any time during the school year.

Equity, access, and opportunity must drive assessment. Racial, cultural, and linguistic factors should be considered when deciding on what type of tests to use and who should administer them. Curriculum and instruction should be determined by collaboration among specialists in the fields of gifted education, special education, assessment, curriculum, and instruction.

Cultural Responsive Teaching provides a framework to ensure the integration of cultural norms, traditions, and values into the teaching and learning experience. The educators in this field also stress the importance of teaching to the students' strengths, referred to as a "strength-based perspective." Curricular materials must be developed by and for diverse cultural groups. It must ensure representational and authentic imagery, literature, and traditions.

Native American, African American, Asian American, Caucasian, Hispanic American, Latino, Middle Eastern, and all first-generation immigrants must be included in all aspects of the curriculum and instruction. Cross-cultural experiences help teachers to create meaningful relationships with their students.

Erinn Fears Floyd writes

> Decades of research and history have shown a staggering disparity in the representation of Black students and white students in Gifted and Talented (GATE) programs across the country. There are glaring inequities in Gifted and Talented programs as Black students are not referred, assessed, or offered entry at the same rate as white students.

While there is the rallying cry that Black Lives Matter, the reality of the lack of minority students in GATE programs begs the question, "Do Black Lives Matter?" It is imperative that the stark reality of this question be addressed honestly and with a *call to action*. It should include policy, programming, and practices in schools and school districts that provide access and equity for all students.

As challenging is the identification of 2e and 3e students in the Caucasian population, it is even more so among the black population. In addition, the 3e students come from substandard schooling environments, low-income, and poverty homes. Educators must understand the linguistic, cultural, and racial differences from their own where they exist in order to understand their students and to create a positive learning environment in their classrooms.

We must face and address the hard reality Jackie Spinner wrote about in *The Washington Post*.

> I only knew that being different and Black in America means that my son is vulnerable if stopped by the police. A 2016 report, analyzing incidents

from 2013-2015, found that nearly half the people killed by police had some sort of disability. A 2019 study of police-involved deaths found 1 in every 1,000 Black Men at risk of being killed by law enforcement.

Jackie Spinner is the parent of a neurologically diverse son and associate professor at Columbia College in Chicago. She presented hard facts that require a *call to action* by educators and professionals in the fields of policy and government. All three exceptionalities, giftedness, learning disability, and racial must be addressed in order for appropriate intervention to take place.

Biased, unfair tests that prevent black students from being identified as *gifted* must be replaced by unbiased, fair tests that identify black students for Gifted and Talented Programs.

This will allow a greater number of black students to actually be in the Gifted and Talented (GATE) classrooms and eliminate the feeling of being alone and isolated in those programs.

Whether an education major, a classroom teacher, a school administrator, a parent, or a concerned citizen, the call for racial justice must be heeded. Stephanie Coxon writes "It is imperative that we all commit ourselves to building a world where the marginalized are liberated from systemic oppression. The time to do the work is now."

We must start by recognizing and addressing our own biases. Only then can we move forward to educate ourselves about the injustices faced by so many. There are ways to advocate for social justice in the community. We must all speak out against racist behavior wherever and whenever it might occur.

This is part of the challenge we face in order to address the urgent needs of thrice exceptional students. The recognition of thrice exceptional students is relatively new but there is some excellent research being conducted in the field which must be put into practice in the classroom.

Teacher education programs can have a very positive impact on the preparation of teachers who will be able to address the academic needs of both twice exceptional and thrice exceptional students.

CHAPTER 7. THRICE EXCEPTIONAL STUDENTS' CHALLENGES

Post

EDUCATORS: CLASS DISCUSSION

1. Discuss how you plan to address the needs of your thrice exceptional students based on your reading of this chapter.

2. Compare and contrast the various types of thrice exceptional students.

PARENTS

1. Discuss how you plan to advocate on behalf of your thrice exceptional child based on your reading of this chapter.

2. Describe the school environment you expect for your 3e child. Has this expectation been met?

3. How? Or why not?

4. What specific needs do you continue to expect to be met for your 3e child?

Chapter 8

"Thou Shalt Not Bully"

INTRODUCTION

EDUCATORS

1. Describe how you plan to create a bully-free classroom.

2. Discuss the importance of having students participate in the creation of a bully-free classroom.

3. Discuss the relationship between bullies and 2e and 3e students.

PARENTS

1. Discuss how parents can support a bully-free classroom.

2. How much do you know about the relationship of bullies and 2e and 3e students?

It has been suggested that if the word bully had existed in Biblical days, we would have a "Thou Shalt Not Bully" commandment. One can find stories about bullying as far back as the Biblical days. If you Google "bullying in the Bible" you will get thousands of hits.

Andy was diagnosed as twice exceptional when he was in the fifth grade. Until then he had been a puzzle to his parents and teachers. *He did so well in certain subjects and poorly in others.* This should have been a clue immediately that he was 2e. He has a wonderful sense of humor, which is a 2e characteristic in some students. He often behaved like the class clown to distract from his academic problems. Andy was one of the most popular students in the class.

A new student, Tom, joined the class in seventh grade and quickly became the class bully with Andy being his prime target. Andy told his parents about his problem with Tom but begged them not to interfere as that would only make the situation worse. However, when the situation got so bad that Andy was waking up in the middle of the night with violent stomach cramps, his parents decided to meet with the school administration.

Fortunately, the administration responded swiftly and effectively. They met with Andy and Tom individually as well as with both sets of parents, separately. Tom was told that all his teachers had been alerted to observe his behavior and any sign of bullying would result in suspension. During Tom's meeting, he told the principal that he was being bullied at home by his high school-age stepbrothers. His parents had no idea that this was going on.

Andy's story underscores the importance of exploring the reasons that the bully is behaving in that manner. Intervention is often needed on behalf of the bully as well as the target/victim. The boys continued through school, graduating high school together. They were never close friends, but they learned to understand one another.

Given all those twice exceptional students must deal with, they certainly don't need to be forced to deal with bullies as well. Yet students who are perceived as different by their classmates often become the targets/victims of bullies. Twice exceptional and thrice exceptional students are frequently perceived as different. In many classrooms, there are students who are very protective of their special needs classmates, but in other classrooms bullies try to take over.

Originally the targets of bullies were called victims. It was determined that the term victim indicated that the person had no way out, no escape. Therefore, the term target was added to demonstrate that in some cases the person may be targeted by the bully, but he/she may, in fact, defy the bully's intentions.

Gifted and talented students do have special needs. We tend to equate special needs only to students who are physically, academically, or neurologically challenged but gifted and talented students deserve extra attention, especially when it comes to bullying. More than two-thirds of academically talented eighth graders say they had been bullied at school and almost one-third harbored violent thoughts as a result, according to a study believed to be the first to examine the prevalence and impact of bullying in a group some experts regard as particularly vulnerable (see table 8.1).

A valuable tool to create a bully-free environment for all students is SuEllen Fried's Student Empowerment Session. It is described in detail in *Banishing Bullying Behavior: Transforming the Culture of Peer Abuse*, a book that SuEllen Fried and I coauthored in a chapter titled *"Empowering Students in the Solution."* It is described in enough detail that all educators can apply this hour-long program in their classrooms successfully.

Fried stresses the importance of following the program she created more than two decades ago exactly as described. She has presented her Student Empowerment Session to more than 60,000 students in 36 states. Fried and all presenters such as this author open the session by introducing themselves and telling Kim's story.

Kim was an eleven-year-old terminally ill cancer patient who was bullied on the playground during recess by boys who pulled off her wig and laughed at her bald head. Here she was fighting for her life, and she had to fight bullies as well. Kim's story is so compelling that every child in the room is caught up in it. You can hear a pin drop and the students are ready to participate when Fried tells them that she wants to learn about bullying from them.

Fried stresses that using the Socratic method of asking questions is an absolutely essential part of the process. All questions should be open-ended and allow for a multitude of answers. The questions should be prepared in advance and presented in a particular order beginning with physical bullying. Students shout out answers like poking, shoving, hitting, tripping, and punching.

Less frequently mentioned are urinating on someone, swirly (forcing someone's head into the toilet and flushing the toilet — a favorite in the boy's restroom), shooting, and stabbing. Any type of physical contact that can be hurtful and inflict pain is considered to be physical bullying.

The SES then moves on to verbal bullying that includes any use of words to hurt the target. It is suggested that if one changes the well-known sticks and stones to "Sticks and stones can break your bones, but words can break your heart," one can conclude that broken bones can usually heal much faster than a broken heart.

Making fun of disabilities, spreading rumors, mimicking, whispering, sarcasm, and put-downs are all examples students contribute to the discussion of verbal bullying.

The discussion then turns to emotional bullying, that is nonverbal aggression such as pointing, staring, exclusion, rejection, ostracizing, turning your back on someone. It is the most difficult to describe because it is intangible and considered to be the most painful. Students discuss being excluded from playgroups during the early elementary school year, excluded from being allowed to sit at a certain lunchroom table and other gatherings.

Fried frequently shares Tanya's story.

> Tanya's story is repeated time and again in the lives of twice exceptional and thrice exceptional students. Their "differentness" often makes them targets and exclusion is a form of emotional bullying that is used. This very painful form of bullying is found on the continuum of bullying behavior from early childhood through senior adulthood.

Next in the order of the Student Empowerment Session is a discussion of sympathy, empathy, and apologies which have to be more than "I am sorry" but include the promise that the bullying behavior will not be repeated. The teacher then asks whether there is anyone brave enough to make an apology. Usually, several hands go up and apologies can go back for behavior that took place many years earlier such as an apology in sixth grade for an episode that took place in kindergarten.

Students are then asked if they accept the apology, and the answer is usually in the affirmative.

Table 8.1   Types of Bullying

PHYSICAL BULLYING	Poking, shoving, hitting, tripping, and punching are usually shouted out by students. (Less frequently mentioned are urinating on someone, swirly, shooting, and stabbing.) *Any type of physical contact that can be hurtful and inflict pain is considered physical bullying.*
VERBAL BULLYING	Making fun of disabilities, spreading rumors, mimicking, whispering, sarcasm, and put-downs. *Verbal bullying includes any use of words to hurt the target.*
EMOTIONAL BULLYING	Nonverbal aggression such as pointing, staring, exclusion, rejection, ostracizing, and turning your back on someone. (Students discuss being excluded from playgroups during early elementary school years and/or excluded from being allowed to sit at a certain lunchroom table and other gatherings.) *It is the most difficult to describe because it is intangible and considered to be the most painful.*

The hour-long session ends on a very positive note and research has documented the efficacy of the Student Empowerment Session. Twice exceptional students don't need the pain inflicted by bullies in addition to the burden their exceptionalities place on them.

All students are the beneficiaries of the Student Empowerment Session. Creating a bully-free environment in the classroom enhances the learning environment. Having experienced the powerful impact of the SES, I strongly urge all educators to learn how to conduct these sessions for the benefit of all their students. The author hopes that this brief summary of the Student Empowerment Session will encourage all teachers to read the chapter that will enable them to implement this very powerful classroom program.

Twice exceptional students may also become bullies. The pain inflicted on them as the result of being bullied sometimes causes them to bully. Adults have reported that when they were younger and in pain caused by some traumatic event in their lives, such as divorce or a family death, they felt that if they inflicted pain on others, it might lessen their own pain.

The addition of being a target/victim of bullying to being twice exceptional brings these individuals to the level of 3e, thrice exceptional. The third exceptionality requires as much intervention as do the first two. Again, it must be stressed that twice exceptional students are often perceived as different and therefore become targets/victims of bullies.

Seven mothers tell the heartbreaking stories of how unbearable bullying led to the suicide of their children in a book compiled by Brenda High: *Bullycide in America: Moms Speak Out About the Bullying/ Suicide Connection.* She published this book to build awareness of how serious bullying is and with the hope that education about this topic would prevent future tragedies.

Cathy Swartwood Mitchell, Brandon Chris Swartwood's mother, chronicled years of torture by a group of bullies. She describes in great detail the frustration caused by the family's inability to get the school administration to intervene and their inability to get proper legal help. For many years she followed the court records of the perpetrators. At least three of them had numerous felony charges or convictions for some of their crimes.

All three had some protective orders filed against them by their spouses or girlfriends. Other charges include possession of controlled substances, multiple burglaries, domestic abuse, and child abuse. Cathy actually attended a number of the bullies' trials. She concluded, "As students they were liars, thieves, thugs and abusers. Now these school bullies, in adulthood, they are societies' criminals."

It is clear that *bullying* is not a phase. Children and teens don't grow out of being bullies just because they reach a certain age. It is also clear that bullying does not just happen. It is estimated that approximately 50 percent of the students who are bullies at school are bullied at home by either parents or siblings.

Bullying is a continuum from early childhood through senior adulthood often passed on from one generation to the next. The only way to break the cycle is by recognizing it and addressing it with appropriate intervention. In order to do so, it is crucial to understand and identify bullying at all stages of the life-long continuum, and in a variety of settings such as in twice exceptional students' schools. It is also crucial to address the needs of the bully.

For many generations bullying was considered "a rite of passage," the province of playground activities. "Hot Spots" have always included the school bus, the lunchroom, the boys' and girls' restrooms, gym locker rooms, and any other venue the bullies could find to torture their targets/victims.

More than one alert janitor was well aware of who the bullies were and what they were up to in their schools. When these janitors saw the bullies enter the restroom they would quickly follow with their buckets and mops and head off any bullying behavior.

Electronic/Cyberbullying has become the most recent form of this age-old source of human pain. Cyberbullying occurs in many forms (see table 8.2).

Table 8.2   Types of Cyber Bullying

ANONYMITY	The internet allows the cyberbully to remain completely unknown to the target/victim by using aliases or pseudonyms.
CYBER STALKING	Cyber stalking is considered a form of harassment. Targets/victims often fear that online stalking will actually escalate to live stalking.
DENIGRATION	Denigration is often referred to as online "dissing." The bully spreads lies, rumors, and gossip designed to harm the target's/victim's reputation.
EXCLUSION	Exclusion is one of the most painful forms of bullying at any age. In the case of cyberbullying, it is simply excluding someone from an online group.
FLAMING	Flaming is a heated argument online through instant messaging or by e-mail. Offensive language is often used, as well as capital letters.
HARASSMENT	Harassment occurs when messages of a threatening nature are posted online or sent to a target/victim twenty-four hours a day.
IMPERSONATION	Perpetrators go online as someone else with material and/or messages to get the person they are impersonating into trouble. Impersonation is also known as masquerading and posing.
OUTING	Outing is the public display or forwarding of personal communication. It is often sexual information that has been shared in the belief that it will be held in the strictest of confidence.
TRICKERY	Trickery is used to get someone to reveal secret information, that is then shared online. *Outing* can be a product of *trickery* and often is.

ANONYMITY

The very nature of the internet offers anonymity to anyone who wants to hide his or her identity. It allows the cyberbully to remain completely unknown to the target/victim by using aliases or pseudonyms.

Jacqui suddenly started to receive messages all signed by Ella. She didn't know anyone by that name. Jacqui was a twice exceptional middle-school student with a small group of friends and no known enemies, but the messages kept coming. The same message time after time, "You are so ugly. You should kill yourself." Jacqui had no idea as to what prompted these messages and after several years of relentless cyberbullying, she committed suicide.

CYBER STALKING

Cyber stalking is considered a form of harassment. Targets often fear that online cyber stalking will actually escalate to live stalking. Although not all cases of cyber stalking become "live" stalking, enough do that the fear should be taken seriously.

Cyber stalking often takes place via e-mail and text messages. The perpetrators are relentless about the message of choice again, which is "You are so ugly. You should kill yourself." And all too often tragically these victims do commit suicide.

DENIGRATION

Denigration is often referred to as online "dissing." The bully spreads lies, rumors, and gossip designed to harm the victim's reputation. Among teenagers, this is used to break up friendships and relationships. Denigration can be the cause of a tremendous amount of pain when successfully carried out by the bully.

EXCLUSION

As discussed earlier, the pain inflicted by bullies often lasts a lifetime. Exclusion is one of the most painful forms of bullying at any age. In the case of cyberbullying, it is simply excluding someone from an online group and thereby causing the target/victim a great deal of pain. Twice exceptional and thrice exceptional individuals are often very sensitive and finding themselves excluded is very hurtful.

Exclusion has long been an issue at summer sleep-away camps. However, before the existence of the internet, once the camp season was over, bullying was a matter of the past. Now the exclusion continues year-round on the internet.

This form of bullying starts in early childhood and can be found in senior citizen settings. In preschool, children are often heard to say, "You can't play with us." Throughout school exclusion from the lunchroom table occurs over and over again as it does in retirement communities. In all instances appropriate intervention is crucial.

FLAMING

Flaming is a heated argument online through instant messaging or by e-mail. Offensive language is often used, as well as capital letters. The highly publicized case of bullying by Miami Dolphins player Richie Incognito of his teammate Jonathan Martin included a tremendous amount of cyberbullying, much of it flaming. These were covered in a great deal of detail by the press from coast to coast. The offensive language going back and forth between the two players was shocking, and in the not-too-distant past would have been considered "not fit to print."

HARASSMENT

Harassment occurs when messages of a threatening nature are posted online or sent to a target/victim twenty-four hours a day. These messages are often posted on all sorts of social media. Although harassment does occur among students, it is more frequently used by adults, especially in the workplace.

IMPERSONATION

The perpetrators of this type of cyberbullying go online as someone else with material and messages to get the person they are impersonating into trouble. They might also try to get a third person into trouble. The messages or posts might put the target/victim in danger or damage his or her reputation.

Many examples of impersonation have been reported by the press when it has led to serious damage to reputations, friendships, and relationships. Sometimes impersonation has consequences as serious as bullycide. This form of cyberbullying is also called *masquerading and posing*.

OUTING

Outing is another form of cyberbullying that has taken a tremendous toll on its targets/victims. It is the public display or forwarding of personal communication. It is often sexual information that someone has shared with a friend in the belief that it will be held in the strictest confidence. The most frequent venues for outing are text messages, e-mail, and instant messaging.

Outing can cause serious psychological damage and can lead to self harming behaviors, including suicide. Tyler Clementi's tragic story is a well-known example of outing. An accomplished and very talented violinist, he began the process of coming out the summer after high school. But his roommate expedited the process by outing him online to his new peers at Rutgers University, which led to Tyler's suicide.

TRICKERY

Trickery is used to get someone to reveal secret information, which is then shared online. It is painful for the target/victim on two counts: first, because the target/victim feels betrayed by someone he/she thought could be trusted, second, because of the consequences brought about once the information has been made public. *Outing* can be a product of *trickery* and often is.

There is no doubt that cyberbullying can play a serious role in the lives of twice exceptional students making them thrice exceptional. We will discuss the important role that parents and teachers can play in chapter 10, Parent-Teacher Partnership.

CHAPTER 8. "THOU SHALT NOT BULLY"

Post

EDUCATORS

1. Describe any additions you might make as you create a bully-free classroom.

2. Discuss the importance of having students participate in the creation of a bully-free classroom.

3. Discuss the relationship between bullies and 2e and 3e students.

PARENTS

1. Describe any additional thoughts on how parents can support a bully-free classroom.

2. How will you put what you know about the relationship of bullies and 2e and 3e students into action?

Chapter 9

Parent-Teacher Partnership

INTRODUCTION

EDUCATORS

1. Discuss the importance of the teacher-parent partnership.

2. Outline how you plan to create this partnership.

3. Describe how you plan to implement the teacher-parent partnership.

PARENTS

1. Describe how you plan to participate in the teacher-parent partnership.

2. Discuss the importance of this partnership from the parents' perspective.

3. How do you plan to advocate for your child?

Matt's teacher called his mother and said,

> Betty, I have been debating for three months as to whether to tell you this, but I am concerned and think you should know about an episode in class. We had a discussion about love and Matt said he felt loved by his parents when he was punished. I thought you might want to have him talk to a professional to see if something is going on.

Needless to say, Matt's mother was upset by the call and immediately called Matt's pediatrician for guidance. In his infinite wisdom, Dr. Pakula suggested that she ask Matt about the statement. At first, he was puzzled by the question, after all the discussion had been held three months ago. "Oh, now I remember! I said, 'I feel loved even when I am being punished.'"

What a difference one word makes! Betty was concerned about the possibility that Matt's teacher had been looking at him as a disturbed student all these months. They were personal friends in addition to the parent-teacher relationship. Betty was grateful that the issue had been resolved in such a positive fashion. She was grateful for Dr. Pakula's usual sage advice.

Matt's response is a perfect example of a child who feels his parents' unconditional love. Growing up in home with unconditional love gives children the confidence to face adversarial situations that will come their way.

The parents' role to prepare their children for school begins very early in life. A *Language Arts* textbook, many decades ago, taught Education Majors that infants can tell the difference between a happy voice and an angry voice as early as four months. Thus, if parents raise their voices during an argument, it will have an effect even on the infant.

Thus, early role modeling and teaching are very important in the life of young children and in preparation for appropriate social skills for school. They should be taught when to say "please" and "thank you," how to share and take turns. Children should feel respected and they in turn will respect others.

PARENT ADVOCACY

Parental support and advocacy are extremely important for twice exceptional students. These students often suffer from behavior problems because of the frustration of their situation. For example, Jon, a second grader in a private school was acting out and very disruptive in class.

Teachers and administrators attributed his behavior to "being the youngest very spoiled child" in an upper-income family. However, his parents insisted that Jon have an educational evaluation. The report of the test results indicated that Jon was reading at the eighth-grade level! He was being taught from a second-grade basal reading program. He also had a subtle fine motor problem that kept him from completing writing assignments to his teacher's satisfaction.

Providing Jon with eighth-grade level reading material and adjusting for his fine motor skills deficit eliminated his negative behavior in less than a week. How long could any student, or adult for that matter, endure reading six levels below what he was capable of reading in class day after day without acting out in frustration? Clearly his behavior was a cry for help. Fortunately, his parents responded and advocated on his behalf and both of his 2e issues were addressed.

Acting out behavior in class and/or at home often is a red flag that should alert adults to a child's special needs issues. It is imperative to respond to the symptoms by looking for the cause of the behavior. The parent-teacher partnership can be very helpful in this endeavor.

Another example of parental advocacy was made by Edward's mother on behalf of her very bright 2e high-school son. He was being tutored in math because he continued to fail math quizzes. Edward insisted that he understood the math concepts, though he was unable to pass the math tests. When Edward's mother checked with the math teacher, the instructor confirmed her son's mastery of the math concepts in spite of the math scores.

The mother tried, to no avail, to persuade Edward's teacher to take the student's fine motor issues into consideration. The teacher refused, on the grounds that "it wouldn't be fair to the other students." Edward's mother countered, "But the other students don't have a learning disability!"

Over the years, as we have advocated for twice exceptional and other special needs students from preschool through graduate school we have been told, "But it wouldn't be fair to the other students!" In each case, we have responded, "But the other students don't have a learning disability" and tried to explain the need to intervene in order to help the student to compensate for that disability.

Edward's experience raised the important question of whether we are testing for understanding and knowledge or for the ability to write a quiz. If teachers understand the fact that among students, there is a given population who have deficits for which they must compensate we can avoid many problems and frustrations for these students.

Lina shared her story which underscored how important parent advocacy is and also is a stark example of thrice exceptionality. Her son Calden was born with a number of serious medical issues. Yet, she and her husband observed quite early that Calden had an "exceptional ability to absorb information and hold onto it."

His kindergarten teacher and special education teacher both recognized his outstanding intelligence met his intellectual needs. They were surprised to learn that one of the apps that Calden had to use in class did not recognize him because it did not take people of color into account. Lina said bluntly, "(It's) definitely a mode of systemic racism and we need to accept it exists." But it must be a *call to action* that is heeded!

By the time Calden reached third grade he was placed in fifth-grade math, reading, and science classes. However, a change of administration brought in a principal who was overheard using racial and disability names for Calden and questioning why he should be in these advanced classes. Lina continued to advocate for Calden to receive the academic program based on the testing results.

The administration was so uncooperative that she and her husband had to resort to engaging an education attorney. Lina shared that her faith had been a "strong anchor" throughout this long ordeal until they found the Flex School, where Calden is reported to be very happy with his academic needs being met. His third exceptionality, being a student of color, represents what many students of color have to deal with.

Line leaves us with some very sage advice:
- You know your child best. You *are* the expert on your child.
- *Never give up.* Dedicate yourself to advocacy and rise above perceptions you can't control as "angry Black woman/man."
- *Educate* yourself on the system, and live respectfully, true to who you are.
- *Identify* partners in the school system that believe and care.
- *Accept that systemic racism exists* in technology and curricula, be alert and protect your child.

This advice should be heeded by all parents. Unfortunately, it is based on years of experience by a woman who grew up in the Bahamas and found a school system very different from what she expected in the United States. Again, it is a resounding call to action.

Another major area where twice exceptional students need the support and advocacy of parents and teachers is that of bullying, especially cyberbullying. We must remember that special needs students are often viewed as "different" and being different can become the target/victim of a bully.

Both parents and teachers should discuss the very serious dangers involved in cyberbullying with their children and students. If the school has a "no bullying program" it might have some printed material that children can bring home to guide the family discussion. It is very important to communicate the fact that NO personal information should be discussed online. Names, addresses, phone numbers, pictures, passwords, and e-mail should not be given to anyone.

Also, it is very important to set one's privacy settings on Facebook and other social media to select who sees what. Children and students should be taught *not* to open any messages from anyone they do not know.

All bullying messages should be saved, they should not be deleted. These messages are important evidence of cyberbullying whenever it takes place. Keep track of all offensive messages. Google alerts should be set up in your child's name. Google is an excellent source to help deal with cyberbullying or any other form of bullying as well.

Harassment online can be reported by clicking "Help" or "Contact Us" when available by the provider or by submitting a complaint. When physical harm is threatened, the police should be notified. The police should also be notified if mental health is threatened.

Many social networks have security officers who try to take down offensive messages in less than twenty-four hours. This is a vast improvement over earlier attempts to get items removed. In the early days of cyberbullying, it would sometimes take months to have a post taken down. One example is of a Canadian mother who spent eight months trying to get false statements about her son removed to no avail. The statements were out-and-out lies and were very hurtful.

With improved vigilance today, that post would have been removed within a day. Vigilance is very important with regard to bullying and cyberbullying on the part of the school community and the family. Offending messages should be reported immediately.

It is imperative that twice exceptional students do not become targets/victims of bullies. If they do, they become thrice exceptional. A class meeting to discuss the topic of bullying in general with a focus on cyberbullying could be a cooperative effort. The class teacher and classroom mother might host the meeting.

FORMAT FOR CLASS MEETING

Recommend that seating be set up in a circle rather than theater style.

As an "icebreaker" you might invite each person to turn to the person next to them and "interview" them for a few moments to get to know them and then reverse the roles. Rather than going around the room and having each person introduce himself or herself, everyone introduces the person he or she interviewed.

The agenda for the meeting should include:
1. Explanation of the concept of community of learners. This should set a nonthreatening tone for the meeting. Discuss the learning environment you are trying to establish for their children.
2. Discuss the importance of having a bully-free classroom. Give the parents some background on the concept of peer abuse, characteristics of bullies, and ask the parents to be honest with themselves as to whether they see any of these characteristics in their own child.
3. Discuss the importance of working in cooperation with the home and your commitment to do so. In order for this to work successfully, stress to the parents that you need their help. Point out that the research shows the more cooperation between the home and the school, the more successful the student will be and that you know that the parents want to help their children achieve success. (Research has shown that no matter how acrimonious divorce may have been, most divorced couples will come together on behalf of their children.)
4. Also discuss the fact the many parents don't realize that their child is a bully or being bullied; therefore, it is important for them to

know what to look for and how to overcome being a bully or being bullied.

5. The following questions might be presented in the form of a checklist for the parents to ask themselves (see table 9.1):

Does your child:
- Get pleasure from taunting others
- Seek power over others
- Act out anger in physical ways (hitting, kicking, damaging property)
- Become hot-tempered
- Need to be controlling
- Use words to hurt or humiliate other
- Enjoy spreading rumors
- Try to isolate his/her target
- Play on other's insecurity
- Fail to recognize the rights of others
- Lack empathy
- Fail to admit mistakes and correct them
- Lack a sense of humor

Table 9.1   Bullying Checklist for Parents

The following questions might be needed for parents to ask themselves.
Does your child:

Get pleasure from taunting others	
Seek power over others	
Act out in anger in physical ways (hitting, kicking, damaging property)	
Become hot-tempered	
Need to be controlling	
Use words to hurt or humiliate others	
Enjoy spreading rumors	
Try to isolate his/her target	
Play on other's insecurities	
Fail to recognize the rights of others	
Lack empathy	
Fail to admit mistakes and correct them	
Lack a sense of humor	
Has family problems and issues	
Has witnessed abusive behavior	
Has been bullied at school and/or work	
Please add any others:	

- Has family problems and issues
- Has witnessed abusive behavior
- Has been bullied at school and/or at home
- You might ask parents to add to the checklist.

The discussion should then turn to constructive suggestions for addressing these characteristics. Have a list of tools parents can use and explain how you address these issues. Again, asking for parental support and indicating your support for parental actions is very important.

If the class meeting or a meeting with the administrative staff is not an option for you, then the only choice you have is a one-on-one meeting with the parents. It might be helpful for you to speak with your student to ascertain his/her parents' interests such as sports, hunting, fishing, music to try to find a topic of mutual interest to talk about before you start your discussion on the topic of bullying.

PARENT PARTICIPATION

Although there was no formal assessment of a correlation between parent participation and student success in the University of Missouri-Kansas City Reading Clinic, the faculty reported that they found on the whole students whose parents participated in the program were more successful. There are many opportunities for parents to participate in their children's classrooms.

Teachers can always use the assistance of a tutor for students who would benefit from one-on-one help. They can use help with preparing materials for instruction. Guest readers for story time are very welcome. The role of Room Mother has always been important. Volunteering to go on field trips can be an excellent opportunity to get to know the class dynamics.

Having two to four parent meetings each year can certainly enhance the parent-teacher partnership. It should be an opportunity to have positive programs and build relationships. Organizing such programs might be part of the job of the Room Mother or the teacher might recruit two sets of parents to co-chair each program and they in turn would recruit a committee to plan the program and provide refreshments.

An example of an effective program is giving the parents five to ten minutes to jot down how they envision the school five years hence. The program can be facilitated by a parent skilled at that or by an outside facilitator. Each parent then shares his/her thoughts without duplicating what has already been said.

The facilitator often gives prompts while the parents are writing such as "What happens as the students arrive in the morning? What are the students doing in the lunchroom? What has been updated in terms of equipment?"

The group might break for refreshments and socializing while the facilitator puts the responses into a cohesive narrative to present to the group. This type of brainstorming allows parents to think about the possibilities of the future of their children's education.

Much has been written about Executive Functions and Executive Skills. Many schools have counselors who coach students in specific functions and skills they might be lacking. There are also professional coaches available outside of school for students who need more extensive coaching in this area. Parents should be informed of these deficits by the classroom teacher so that they can also help their children master these skills.

An interpreter should be available for parents who are recent immigrants at parent-teacher conferences so that there can be excellent communication between the parents and teachers, allowing parents to ask any questions they might have. This is an important accommodation for the parents of thrice exceptional students.

Students learn English as their second language much faster than their parents do. On average, students master English in their classroom within four months. Students who learned to read in their native tongue learn to read English much faster than nonreaders.

CHAPTER 9. PARENT-TEACHER PARTNERSHIP

Post

EDUCATORS: CLASS DISCUSSION

1. Discuss the importance of the teacher-parent partnership.

2. Outline how you plan to create this partnership.

3. Discuss how you plan to implement the teacher-parent partnership.

PARENTS

1. Describe how you plan to participate in the teacher-parent partnership based on your reading of this chapter.

2. Discuss the continued importance of this partnership from the parents' perspective.

3. How will this partnership help you to advocate for your child?

Chapter 10

Creating a Path to Success for Twice Exceptional Students

INTRODUCTION

EDUCATORS

1. Describe the pathway to success.

2. Make a road map to create a pathway to success.

3. Discuss several different road maps to success.

PARENTS

1. Describe the pathway that led to your child's success.

2. What were the most important factors that led to your child's success?

Larry, a high-school junior, is a bright, socially skilled, and highly capable young adult. He has earned a reputation as an extraordinarily talented musician. However, his academic record clearly shows a record of underperformance, and Larry has experienced frustration. Concerned that Larry is not nearly achieving his academic potential, his parents arranged for Larry to have a Neuropsychological Evaluation.

Larry's situation was exacerbated by COVID-19, which forced his appointment to be delayed for a year and a half, causing him further frustration. His problems with activities entailing attentional, organizational, time management, and task initiation skills date back many years. Both his parents and teachers suspected that he has ADHD.

During the long-delayed meeting with the psychologist, Larry's parents described him "as an incredibly bright, responsible and independent young man with sophisticated reasoning skills." They called him enormously creative, someone who "thinks outside the box." Larry also has a strong knack for complex technological activities. He enjoys dissecting, repairing, and operating iPhones and drones. "He even built a computer-on his own-just a few months ago," they added.

At the same time, Larry has long-standing weaknesses in related areas of *attention and executive functioning*. As discussed earlier, every 2e and 3e student is different, even as they often share certain identifying characteristics. It is interesting to note some of the classic 2e characteristics that Larry exhibits.

Larry's parents shared that he has a long history of *zoning out, daydreaming, and needs reminders to turn in his assignments*. He can be *moody at times*, especially when he feels overwhelmed academically. With this description of a clearly gifted and talented student with ADHD one wonders why his school had not identified him as twice exceptional much earlier.

Larry's father shared that Larry demonstrated musical intelligence and musical aptitude as early as his toddler years. However, he was also prone to *procrastination, inattention, and organizational problems*. These problems were noted by teachers as well. Again, we are left with the question, why was Larry not identified much earlier as 2e?

The Educational Evaluation characterized Larry both as "refreshingly laid back and even keeled" as well as hardworking. He demonstrated strong social skills, made good eye contact, "read" and responded to nonverbal social communication effectively, and was easily engaged in conversation. With his natural musical talent, Larry has what Howard Gardner identifies as "Musical Intelligence."

When an individual has been identified as twice exceptional, many clinicians no longer report a Full-Scale IQ since the learning disability lowers the true intellectual functioning score of that person. Thus, neither the Full-Scale IQ nor the General Ability Index on the WAIS-IV was reported since they are not a valid indicator of Larry's true abilities.

This approach represents a tremendous improvement over the past interpretation of IQ scores. By not depressing the IQ because of a learning disability, the high subtest scores should qualify 2e students to participate in Gifted/Talented Programs. With participation in special programs for gifted/talented students and remediation for learning disabilities, twice exceptional students should have successful academic experiences.

Larry's high score of sixteen (ten is average) in Similarities and a low score of five in Coding are strong indicators of the exceptionality of Superior intelligence and the exceptionality of a learning disability. Similarities and Vocabulary are the two subtests on the Verbal Scale of the WAIS that test for intellectual intelligence, and Larry scored the highest on both subtests, sixteen and fourteen, respectively. The results validate his giftedness.

His low score of five on both Coding and Symbol Search demonstrates his learning disability. This unevenness of functioning during the testing situation is important for parents and teachers to note to better understand his twice exceptional functioning at home and at school.

Larry's attentional and executive functioning weaknesses have made some academic tasks difficult for him at times. There was a strong recommendation that Larry should receive appropriate academic accommodations.

Larry's diagnosis was ADHD-Predominately Inattentive Presentation, based on findings during the Educational Evaluation that indicated Larry had serious difficulty focusing attention for short intervals as well for longer periods of time. Larry struggled in the area of executive functioning. He demonstrated weakness in planning ability, organizational skills, and working memory.

Larry's performance was variable, and generally weaker than expected, given his Superior intelligence on tests that measure executive functioning. Areas of shortfall include mental control skills that contribute to goal-directed behavior, including inhibition, independent task initiation, set shifting, organization, planning, and cognitive flexibility. These are clearly a strong indicator of his learning disability.

Executive functioning skills enable students to plan and achieve goals. The basic skills are proficiency in adaptable thinking, planning, self-monitoring, self-control, working memory, time management, and organization (see table 10.1).

Table 10.1   Executive Functioning Skills

ADAPTABLE THINKING

The ability to problem-solve, adjust to situations, overcome obstacles, and see things from another's perspective.

PLANNING

The ability to create a plan of action.

SELF-MONITORING

The ability to evaluate their work and make corrections as needed.

SELF-CONTROL

The ability to restrain physical or emotional outbursts, to think before reacting, and remain calm/not shut down when faced with criticism, obstacles, and/or disappointment.

WORKING MEMORY

The ability to retain and store learned information and put it to use.

TIME MANAGEMENT

The ability to make a realistic schedule, complete assignments on time, and allow for productivity and punctuality.

ORGANIZATION

The ability to arrange materials and thoughts in an orderly way.

SELF-MOTIVATION

The ability to see the reason(s) to do something and then do it.

- *Adaptable thinking* gives student the ability to problem-solve and adjust to situations as they arise. It enables them to overcome obstacles when they arise as well as to see things from another person's perspective.
- *Planning* includes the ability to create a plan of action, such as creating a schedule. It is part of the ability to organize the student's life.

- *Self-monitoring* is an important skill for students to evaluate their work and make corrections as needed. It enables them to see their errors, correct them, learn from them, and move forward.
- *Self-control* is a skill taught in early childhood and crucial to maintain throughout life. It is the student's ability to restrain physical or emotional outbursts. It assures that students will think before they act or react to situations as they arise. Emotional control enables students to remain calm and not overreact or shut down in the face of criticism, obstacles, and disappointment.
- *Working memory* is the student's ability to retain and store learned information and put it to use at a later time. Working memory is a key to academic success.
- *Time management* is the ability to make a realistic schedule, to complete assignments on time, and allows for productivity and punctuality. Once again, it underscores the importance of making and maintaining a schedule.
- *Organization* is the ability to arrange materials and thoughts in an orderly way.
- *Self-motivation* is students' ability to see the reason or reasons to do something and then to get it done.

For the treatment of ADHD, a trial of medication is usually recommended. This issue will be discussed later in this chapter. Many young adults of Larry's age find that short periods of vigorous exercise such as running in place for two minutes or doing twenty pushups before working stimulates their brain enough to help them get started on challenging tasks.

Some classroom teachers have found that playing music and having students walk around their desks for a short period of time is very helpful for all students but especially those with ADHD. Other teachers allow ADHD students to go to the back of the room without disrupting the class and work off their need for movement.

ADHD produces significant functional limitations on students' ability to focus, sustain attention, and to complete tasks within a typical time frame. Specific recommendations for academic accommodations for individuals with ADHD and for each 2e and 3e are key for student's success.

Research has shown that study skills rather than intelligence are the best predictor of which students will be most successful in college. Walter Pauk's "How to Study in College" is now in its eleventh edition! Steps taken by students with good study skills include the following:

Create a schedule:
- Work in well lit, quiet environment with no distractions
- Take time prior to starting work to think through tasks, how much time will they take, and the best task order
- Take breaks to reenergize — time varies according to individual needs
- Break large tasks into shorter segments
- Retaining information is easier when it is meaningful, so contextualize rote information with strategies such as creating associations, visualizations, or other mnemonic strategies

TEST-TAKING ACCOMMODATIONS

Test-taking accommodations are crucial for twice exceptional students to be successful. These students do not learn in the same way that most students do. They differ significantly in the condition, manner, and duration in which they complete tasks in comparison with most students, which is the definition of a disability under the American with Disabilities Act (ADA).

The following accommodations are recommended:

1. At least, 50 percent additional time, 100 percent if needed for quizzes, tests, and exams. This adjustment is especially important for students with impaired planning skills, sustained attention deficits, and slow processing speed.
2. Frequent breaks. Some students just need the breaks to clear and reenergize their minds and may not actually need additional time.
3. Use of a computer or word processor during class, on quizzes, tests, and exams. This accommodation is really important for students with a handwriting problem or with a problem "getting thoughts from their head to paper."
4. When possible, students should have the ability to mark their answers directly into the test booklet rather than an answer sheet because of a tendency to make careless mistakes even when they know correct answers.
5. Use of a four-function calculator when needed.
6. These students should not be penalized for spelling errors, at least not until they have mastered Stopwatch Spelling.

Michael Delman, M.Ed., recognizes the debilitating role anxiety can play in test-taking, especially, math tests. He has shared what he uses in his classes and recommends that parents might want to share this technique with their children's teachers.

> Test phobia seems to be particularly heightened for many students on math tests. For that reason, when I taught math classes, I made it a routine for students to have a moment of quiet calm before we started tests. They would put their heads down, and I would tell them to relax and just notice their breathing and allow it to settle for a moment. I would remind them that they knew as much as they knew, and that they didn't need to impress me or their parents or themselves, that all they needed to do now was to focus on the questions in front of them.
>
> I reminded them of the basic test-taking techniques to use, such as writing down all of the formulas and notes they could remember right away, looking over all the questions before starting, and skipping over the questions that were too hard, and returning later if they had time.
>
> The entire process took only 90 seconds, but in their evaluation of the class, students consistently, taking time to get centered was a huge part of why their math grades improved during the year. Managing their anxiety is such a valuable skill. Without that skill, it is particularly difficult to stay focused in those stressful situations.

This test-taking process may be adapted to any subject matter being taught at any grade level. It is certainly worth ninety seconds to help students get centered and to lower their test-taking anxiety.

Dr. Mel Levine stressed that students like Larry are not "lazy" or unmotivated. He wrote and lectured repeatedly that he had "never met a lazy child!" Rather students with executive functioning difficulty are often very sensitive to the "load" of work they must complete. "Load" consists not only of the amount of work but also the complexity of the work. Anxiety and frustration can add to the "load" and reduce the ability to manage executive functioning demands.

Larry started on the medication prescribed and felt fantastic on the first day. It did everything it was supposed to do. On the second day, he did not feel quite so well, and by the third day he said, "he felt out of his body!" The psychologist recommended a different medication, but Larry decided with the positive results from executive functions coaching he would prefer not to take any medication.

Ritalin was controversial when it was introduced as was the whole concept of medication. For some time, the faculty of the UMKC Reading Clinic would not accept students who were on medication concluding that "Parents and teachers who put children on medication are just too lazy to actually deal with the child." As medical research presented positive scientific studies of the efficacy of medication, the ban was lifted and support for medication grew.

Appropriate medication, usually prescribed by the child's pediatrician, makes it possible for the child to acclimate to the classroom environment. Children are able to control their actions, interactions, and to concentrate on the learning tasks before them.

Two widely used drugs, Concerta and Adderall XR, last long enough to spare the children the embarrassment of having to leave the classroom to go to the nurse to receive a dose of Ritalin that only lasted four to five hours (long-acting Ritalin now lasts for eight hours).

The majority of families who have children diagnosed with ADD and ADHD are grateful for the variety of drugs available to meet the medical needs of their children. The medication debate arose because numerous articles were published about children being medicated unnecessarily. Some parents preferred to *"drugulate"* their children's behavior rather than deal with the causes.

Pediatricians report miraculous effects in their patients who are correctly diagnosed and prescribed medication appropriately. One mother told the author that she refused to accept the fact that her seventh-grade son had ADHD and "fought" the pediatrician about medicating her son. Fortunately, she lost that fight, and her son is one of the miracles pediatricians refer to.

He now is a museum curator, and when I did a follow-up interview, he told me that the medication "saved his academic life." Now he only takes medication when he has tasks that require extraordinary concentration. He still remembers how his pediatrician fought on his behalf and what a difference it made in his life.

Vincent J. Monastra, PhD, devotes an entire chapter on the medication debate in the second edition of *Parenting Children with ADHD: 10 Lessons that Medicine Cannot Teach.* He urges parents to put the question of medication in the context of the child's entire medical treatment for ADHD. He explains the importance of diet and sleep in relation to ADHD and discusses a number of options for parents who are uncomfortable with medication.

However, Dr. Monastra stresses that based on his years of experience in his practice with ADHD children and adults, he has found the most successful treatment is properly administered medication. He urges parents to be sure that any health provider consultant specializes in ADHD.

Another seventh grader, Brad, who had been diagnosed with ADHD a number of years earlier, had responded very well to his medication and enjoyed considerable success in school. Over time, though, his old academic problems gradually returned.

His performance deteriorated to the point that his mother decided to have him evaluated again. The results were the same diagnosis of twice exceptional with the same recommendations. The psychologist urged Brad's mother to have Brad's medication checked periodically. Sure enough, he had "outgrown" the dose he was on, and once that was adjusted, he succeeded academically once again. Medication doses must be checked annually and adjusted as needed.

Larry's story is the story of an untold number of twice exceptional students, students who were identified far deeper into their academic lives than should have been the case. At any point, though, students whose problems are identified appropriately and addressed are able to turn their frustration into success. For Larry, an executive functions coach made all the difference. His ability to use his natural musical talent and musical intelligence is most fulfilling.

This author hopes to be able to publish the second edition of this book filled with success stories of twice exceptional and thrice exceptional students who received identification early, appropriate intervention. That should certainly happen if this call to action is heeded.

CHAPTER 10: CREATING A PATH TO SUCCESS FOR TWICE EXCEPTIONAL STUDENTS

Post

EDUCATORS: CLASS DISCUSSION

1. Discuss the pathway to success after having read this chapter.

2. Make a road map to create a pathway to success after having read this chapter.

3. Compare and contrast several different road maps to success.

PARENTS

1. Describe the pathway that led to your child's success.

2. Discuss the most important factors that led to your child's success?

Appendix A

Assessment of Letter Names Knowledge

This is an example of a very simple instrument that can be administered by parents or teachers to assess whether the student can recognize all the letters of the alphabet. You can duplicate this set of letters or make up one of your own. The key is not to have the letters in alphabetical order and to include all the twenty-six letters, uppercase, and lowercase. Do not put the lowercase *b* and *d* next to each other nor the *p* and *q*.

Have two copies of the letters, one for the student to read from and for you to mark a *check* for correct response and an "X" for an error with the incorrect letter name (see table A.1).

Ask the student to read the letters to you. If the student should ask you whether to read across or down respond "Any way you want." Put an arrow to indicate the direction the student read, across or down. If the student reads down it may indicate that directionality (automatically reading from left to right) has not been established and is another sub-skill of reading that needs practice.

Any letters that are missed must be retaught — one at a time. The most common problems are the confusion of *b* and *d* and *p* and *q*. Each letter should be retaught until mastered and then the next letter retaught.

ASSESSMENT OF LETTER NAME KNOWLEDGE

O H D U F E
A G S T W Z
X L R I N B
C Y P I V Q M K

m h g k w j
q v y a z u
b l c e n s
o d x f i t r p

Table A.1 Assessment of Letter Name Knowledge Checklist

Uppercase Letters									
O		A		X		C		M	
H		G		L		Y		K	
D		S		R		P			
U		T		I		J			
F		W		N		V			
E		Z		B		Q			

Lowercase Letters									
m		q		b		o		r	
h		v		l		d		p	
g		y		c		x			
k		a		e		f			
w		z		n		i			
j		u		s		t			

Appendix B

Stopwatch Spelling

An instructional strategy to teach students one-on-one how to focus or "hold words still in their minds while they learn to spell."

1. Pretest
2. Student reads the spelling list to the teacher. Discuss words to ascertain student's understanding of word meaning. Discussion continues until the student is able to read the list fluently. Note any words that could not be read fluently.
3. Student copies list of words missed on pretest from printed spelling list onto the Focus Time Sheet. The teacher/tutor will then use the Focus Time Sheet to record the period of time the student uses to focus on each spelling word.
4. Stopwatch Spelling is explained to the student as follows: "Pretend that your brain is a camera and that you are going to take a picture of the first word on your spelling list. Tell me when you start to focus, and I will time how long it takes for you to be able to look at the word until you close your eyes and start to spell the word aloud for me. I will then record your time next to the word on the list you copied."
5. If the student cannot spell the word after the first focus, he or she repeats the procedure, and the second focus time is added to the original time recorded. Students quickly learn that it is better to focus a little longer the first time if necessary to see the picture of the word.

6. Student writes the word on the practice sheet, then checks the word against the list. If the word is correct, cover the word and ask the student to write the word once more. The word is learned when the student writes the word correctly twice. If the word is not spelled correctly, repeat focus procedure (step 4) until the word is learned.
7. The procedure is followed until each word on the spelling list of missed words is learned. The procedure is used to learn one word at a time until the list is learned.
8. An oral or written review should take place after every five words.
9. Post-test entire spelling lesson given on the pretest.

References

Adams, D. (1995). *Education for Extinction: American Indians and the Boarding School Experience, 1875–1928*. Lawrence, KS: University Press of Kansas.

Anderson, B.N. (2020). "See Me, See Us": Understanding the Intersections and Continued Marginalization of Adolescent Black Girls in U.S. Classrooms. *Gifted Child Today, 43*(2), 86–100.

Armstrong, T. (1987). *In Their Own Way: Discovering and Encouraging Your Child's Learning Style*. New York: Tarcher/Putnum.

———. (1988). Learning Differences-Not Disabilities. *Principal, 68*(1), 34–36.

Bachtel, K. (2021). Over Here! Seeing Twice-Exceptional Youth in a Neuroblind Society. *Variations 2e, 6*, 34–37.

Carrillo, J.F. (2021). Stories that Know: Barrio Nerds and Intelligences. *Variations 2e, 6*, 18–19.

Castelano, J. (2021). Team Work: Exceptionality (e), 2e, and 3e. *Variations 2e, 6*, 26–30.

Collins, K.H., & Johnson, J.S. (2021). Furthering a Shift in the Twice-Exceptional Paradigm: Understanding the Sociocultural Milieu of Gifted Student Development. *Variations 2e, 6*, 56–60.

Coxon, A. (2021). A Call to Action: Practice Allyship in our Everyday Lives. *Variations 2e, 6*, 48–49.

Davis, J.L., & Cotton, C.R.B. (2021). I'm Gifted Too: Using Culturally Responsive Teaching to Address the Learning Needs of 3e Students. *Variations2e, 6*, 14–17.

Delman, M. (2018). *Your Kid's Gonna Be Okay: A Guide to Raising Competent and Confident Kids*. Needham, MA: Beyond BookSmart, Inc.

Dunbar-Ortiz, R. (2014). *An Indigenous Peoples' History of the United States.* Boston: Beacon Press.

Erinn, F.F. (2021). Shifting the Narrative: Addressing Systemic Racial Disparities of Gifted Students of Color. *Variations 2e, 6,* 38–40.

Fried, S., & Sosland, B. (2009). *Banishing Bullying Behavior: Transforming the Culture of Pain, Rage and Revenge.* Lanham, MD: Rowman and Littlefield Education.

Fried, S., & Sosland, B. (2011). *Banishing Bullying Behavior: Transforming the Culture of Peer Abuse.* 2nd ed. Lanham, MD: Rowman & Littlefield Education.

Gardner, H. (2006). *Multiple Intelligences: New Horizons.* New York: Basic Books.

———. (2011). *Frames of Mind: The Theory of Multiple Intelligences.* New York: Basic Books.

Gentry, M. (2021). Indigenous Youth in Education: Overlooked, Underrepresented, Invisible. *Variations 2e, 6,* 20–25.

Hess, M., & Collins, K.H. (2021). Neither Could He Breathe: Exceptionality, Victimization, and the Death of Elijah McClain. *Variations 2e, 6,* 44–46.

Johnson O'Connor, The Writing Committee. (2021). *Choosing Intelligently: A Practical Guide to Using Your Aptitudes.* Boston: Johnson O'Connor Research Foundation, Human Engineering Laboratory, Inc.

Kang'a, J. (2021). Cradling Different: Thrice exceptional (3e) Voices of Ethnically Diverse Parents. *Variations 2e, 6,* 4–11.

Matranga, S. (2021a). The Cultural and Linguistic Barriers to 2e Identification: Why Latino Students are Being Left Out. *Variation 2e, 6,* 41–43.

Matranga, S. (2021b). Black Brains Matter: Interview with Colin Seale. *Variations 2e, 6,* 54–55.

Mayes, R.D., & Moore III, J.L (2016). The Intersection of Race, Disability, and Giftedness: Understanding the Education Needs of Twice-Exceptional, African American Students. *Gifted Child Today, 39*(2), 98–104.

Monastra, V.J. (2014). *Parenting Children With ADHA: 10 Lessons that Medicine Cannot Teach.* Washington, DC: American Psychological Association.

Silvaroli, N.J. (1978). *Classroom Reading Inventory* (4th ed). Dubuque, IA: WCB/Brown and Company.

Silvaroli, N.J. (1994). *Classroom Reading Inventory* (7th ed). Madison, WI: WCB/Brown and Company.

Sosland, B. (1983). *An Investigation of the Efficacy and Time Efficiency of Using an Individualized Spelling Method on Spelling Achievement When Teaching Spelling to Reading Disabled Students in a Clinic Setting.* Ann Arbor, MI: University Microfilms International.

Sosland, B. (2019). *Banishing Bullying Behavior: A Call to Action from Early Childhood Through Senior Adulthood.* Seattle, WA: Kindle Direct Publishing.

van Gerven, E. (2020). Executive Functions, Executive Skills, and Gifted Learners. In C.M. Fugate, W.A. Behrens, & C. Boswell (Eds.), *Understanding Twice Exceptional Learners: Connecting Research to Practice* (pp. 33–70). Waco, TX: Prufrock Press, Inc.

Wheelock, W., & Campbell, C. (2012). *Classroom Reading Inventory* (12th ed). New York: McGraw Hill.

Whiting, G. (2021). Culture Matters: Race, Gender, and Scholar Identity. *Variations 2e*, 31–33.

Wright, M.J. (1997). Gifted and Learning Disabled. *Learning, 25*(5), 49–51.

Index

Note: Italic page number refer to figures and tables.

adaptable thinking, 96
Adderall XR, 100
ADHD, 94, 95, 97, 100, 101
ADHD-Predominately Inattentive Presentation, 95
advocacy groups, 3
American Indian Alaska Native (AIAN), 64, 65
American with Disabilities Act (ADA), 98
Analytical Reasoning test, 57
anonymity, 77–78
anxiety, 14, 27, 36, 57, 99
Aptitude Teacher Observation Form, 55
aptitude test, 54–58
Armstrong, Thomas, 7
Art Center, 30
"at-risk students," 62
attention-deficit/hyperactivity disorder (ADHD), 27
audiobooks, 2, 3, 40
Auditory Aptitude test, 57

background knowledge, 36
Banishing Bullying Behavior: Transforming the Culture of Peer Abuse (Fried & Sosland), 73–74
Bell, Alexander Graham, 4
Betts, Emmett, 17
Black Lives Matter, 67
black students, 67, 68
bodily-kinesthetic intelligence, 7
bullycide, 80
Bullycide in America: Moms Speak Out About the Bullying/Suicide Connection (High), 75–76
bully-free environment, 73, 75
bullying, 72; anonymity, 77–78; checklist for parents, 89, *89*; cyberbullying, 77, *77*; cyber stalking, 78; denigration, 78; emotional, 74; exclusion, 78–79; flaming, 79; harassment, 79; impersonation, 79–80; life-long continuum, 76; outing, 80; target/victim of, 75; trickery, 80; types of, 73, *73*; verbal, 74
Bureau of Indian Affairs (BIA), 64

Campbell, Connie J., 35, 41
Castellano, Jaime, 66
"The Center Approach," 30
Churchill, Winston, 4
class meeting, format for, 88–90, *89*
Classroom Listening Center, 3
Classroom Reading Inventory (CRI), 17, 35, 37, 41; reading levels, *40*; strengths of, 36
comprehension skills, 36
Clementi, Tyler, 80
Concerta, 100
Coxon, Stephanie, 68
"Cozy Corner"/"The Office"/"Mars," 9
Cruise, Tom, 3
Cultural Responsive Teaching, 67
cyberbullying, 87; types of, 77, *77*
cyber stalking, 78

Delman, Michael, 99
denigration, 78
Dexterity Aptitude test, 58
"Diagnosis and Remediation of Reading Problems in the Classroom," 41, 44
Disney, Walt, 4
distractions, 20, 26
Drama Center, 30

Edison, Thomas, 4, 55
Educational Evaluation, 2, 24, 94, 95
educational needs, twice exceptional students, 9
Education Majors, 84
Einstein, Albert, 6, 7, 55
emotional bullying, 74
end-of-the-year letter, 24
English language, 91
exclusion, 78–79
executive functioning skills, 96, *96*
eye contact, 21, 27, 94

Falker, George, 4
flaming, 79
Floyd, Erinn Fears, 67
Focus Time Sheet, 46, *48, Appendix*
Foresight test, 57
Fried, SuEllen: *Banishing Bullying Behavior: Transforming the Culture of Peer Abuse*, 73–74
frustration, 2, 3, 14–16, 41, 50, 76, 85, 86, 94, 99, 101
Frustration Level, 38–39
Full-Scale IQ, 95

Gardner, Howard, 6, 8; "multiple intelligences," 21
Gifted and Talented (GATE) programs, 28–29, 65, 67, 68
gifted/talented students, 2, 4
Google, 87
Graphoria test, 58
Grip test, 58

harassment, 79; online, 87
High, Brenda: *Bullycide in America: Moms Speak Out About the Bullying/Suicide Connection*, 75–76
Hoopa Valley Indian Reservation (HVIR), 66
Howard Gardner's Multiple Intelligences, 6, 7, 9, 58
"How to Study in College" (Pauk), 97–98
hyperactivity, 27

Ideaphonia test, 56
identified gifted child, 16
identified learning-disabled child, 16
illegible handwriting, 21
impersonation, 79–80
incidental observation, 17
Independent Level, 37–38, 40

independent reading, 37
Independent Reading Level, 29
Independent Research Project, 30
Indian Education Act (1972), 64
Indian Self-Determination Act (1975), 64
Individuals with Learning Disabilities Educational Act (IDEA), 4
Inductive Reasoning test, 57
Informal Reading Inventory (IRI), 3, 14, 17, 34, 35, *38*, *39*, 45
Instructional Level, 3, 38–40
intelligence: bodily-kinesthetic, 7; interpersonal, 7; intrapersonal, 7–8; linguistic, 6; logical-mathematical, 6, 8; musical, 7, 8; naturalist, 8
Interest test, 58
interpersonal intelligence, 7
intrapersonal intelligence, 7–8

Johnson O'Connor Research Foundation, 54–55, *56*, 58; aptitude test, 54–55

K-12 students, 4

language development, 36, 37
Language Experience Approach, 20, 26–27
Lara-Cooper, 66
Latino students, 64, 66
learners, identification with diverse needs, 2
Learning Centers, 30, 31
learning disability, 3, 4, 9, 14–16, 63, 95
learning-disabled students, 2
learning to spell, *45*, 45–46
letter names knowledge assessment, 103–4, *104*

Levine, Mel, 99
linguistic intelligence, 6, 58
Listening Capacity, 14, 17; score, 41
Listening Capacity Level, 3, 39, *39*
listening center, 9
literacy center, 30
logical-mathematical intelligence, 6, 8

math anxiety, 27
Maxwell, Graham S., 16–17
mnemonics, 26
Moby Dick, 2
Monastra, Vincent J., 100–101
musical intelligence, 7–9, 94, 95, 101

naturalist intelligence, 8
"no bullying program," 87
nonverbal IQ tests, 64
Numerical Aptitude test, 57

observation, 16–17
O'Connor, Johnson, 54–58
offensive language, 79
offensive messages, 87
online harassment, 87
oral language, 2, 5, 6
organization, 97
outing, 80

parent advocacy, 84–88
parent participation, 90–91
parent-teacher partnership, 85; class meeting format, 88–90, *89*; parent advocacy, 84–88; parent participation, 90–91
Park University, 14
Pauk, Walter: "How to Study in College," 97–98
pediatricians, 100
phonics, 20, 26
planned observation, 17

planning, 96
Polacco, Patricia, 3, 4, 8–9

race, 63–64
Reading Clinic students, 36
reading levels: Classroom Reading
    Inventory, 39, *40*; criteria for,
    35; Frustration Level, 38–39;
    Independent Level, 37–38, 40;
    Instructional Level, 3, 38–40;
    Listening Capacity Level, 3,
    38–40
reading practice, 37
recognition skills, 36
remedial reading program, 2
Ritalin, 100
Rockefeller, Nelson, 3
Room Mother, 90

Sabatino, Carl, 64
Science Center, 30
second-grade reading level, 14
self-control, 96–97
self-monitoring, 96
self-motivation, 97
Sherk, John, 44, 62
Silograms test, 57–58
Silvaroli, Nicholas, 17, 35
social networks, 87
spatial intelligence, 6
special educations, students in, 3
Spelling Survey, 41
spelling words, 20, 26, 27; practice
    writing, 48, *49*
Spinner, Jackie, 67–68
stalking, 78
Stopwatch Spelling, 45, 46, 105–6;
    Focus Time Sheet, 46, *48*; post-
    test, 48, *50*; pretest, 46–47, *47*
Structural Visualization test, 55
Student Empowerment Session
    (SES), 73–75

students: K-12, 4; in special
    educations, 3; thrice exceptional.
    See thrice exceptional (3e)
    student; twice exceptional. *See*
    twice exceptional (2e) students
Superior intelligence, 95

teacher education programs, 37, 68
"Teacher Observation in Student
    Assessment," 16
Tesla, Nikola, 55
"Test of Letter Knowledge," 44
test-taking accommodations, 98–101
Thorndike (Professor), 17, 34, 35
three-step process, 62, *63*
thrice exceptional (3e) students, 63,
    65; AIAN, 64, 65; identification
    of, 67; nonverbal IQ tests, 64;
    race, 63–64; recognition of, 68;
    targets/victims of bullies, 72–73
time management, 97
trickery, 80
twice exceptional (2e) students,
    2–3; academic needs of, 15;
    categories of, 16; characteristics
    and behaviors, 17, *18–19*,
    20–21; characteristics of,
    5; educational needs, 9; eye
    contact, 21; identification
    of, 14–17; interventions for,
    24–31, *29*; natural aptitudes,
    54–58; parent advocacy, 84–88;
    strengths and weaknesses of,
    5–10, *7*; targets/victims of
    bullies, 72–73; test-taking
    accommodations, 98–101

unidentified child, 16
United States, schools for twice
    exceptional students, 9

verbal bullying, 74

vigilance, 88
Visual Aptitude test, 57
visualization, 26, 27, 45, 46
Vocabulary test, 58

Washington, George, 3
Wechsler Intelligence Tests, 58

Wheelock, Warren H., 35, 41
white students, 64, 67
Wiebe, Chris, 64
Wilson, Woodrow, 3
"word caller," 36
working memory, 97
Workplace Personality test, 58

About the Author

Blanche E. Sosland, PhD, is the coauthor of two books on banishing bullying behavior and the author of a third book, *Banishing Bullying Behavior: From Early Childhood Through Senior Adulthood.* Her work as an educator and clinician focused on twice exceptional children and adults.

She is professor emerita, Park College, Parkville, Missouri. Dr. Sosland earned her BA from Barnard College, Columbia University, and her doctorate from the University of Missouri, Kansas City. She and her husband Neil live in Kansas City, Missouri, and share a home with their adult children in Cotuit, Massachusetts.